The Full and Complete
Unedited Biography and Memoir
of the Amazing Life and Times
# of Randy S.!

Written and Typed by Noah B.

SUNSHINE BEAM PUBLISHING

A SUNSHINE BEAM BOOK

Sunshine Beam Books are published
by Sunshine Beam Publishing Inc.,
Poolesville, Maryland 20837

Design by Randy S.
Written by Randy S. and Noah B.

First Printing, January 2, 2016
Second Printing, September 11, 2018

Printed in the U.S.A. Proudly!

Let Randy know if you would like for
him to come to your bookclub:
Numberonelover453@yahoo.com

INTRODUCTION

In the fall of 2017, while visiting my family in suburban Maryland, I stopped at a garage sale, in Poolesville, about thirty miles west of Washington, D.C.

At these sales, I tend to pore over LPs, books, old postcards, and any other interesting gimcrack or geegaw that catches me ol' fancy. I'll typically purchase at least one item. An old VHS tape. A "Best Of" LP from a 1970s rocker that I could always hear on the radio for free, if I ever had any inclination to do so, which I usually don't. A clock shaped like a Maryland crab. A "gently worn" Baltimore Orioles T-shirt. *Anything. Just one damn thing. Don't be rude, Mike. Buy something!*

So, at this particular sale, I bought something. Specifically: a book.

It was at the bottom of a large cardboard box, beneath a dozen or so moldering issues of *National Geographic* and *Smithsonian Magazine*, two essential publications in any D.C.-area home.

I flipped through the book.

It felt a bit *off*.

Way off.

Awful.

Was this an elaborate joke? An art school project? What in the hell *was* this, exactly? A work of genius by a writer with Nabokovian pretentions? A work of garbage by a writer with Nabokovian pretentions? I was confused. How did the owner first come across it?

I asked. He didn't remember. Neither did his two teenage children. *Maybe from a library book sale? Or from the church flea market?* Shrugs.

The manuscript resembled a "book" that an author could zip off at a Kinko's or create by slipping an endless stream of quarters into the copying machine at a local library. The spiral binding was of the cheap plastic variety, the type used for company employee manuals or the menus at 24-hour Greek diners.

Beneath the lengthy title of the book was a photograph of a young-ish man I assumed had to be this "Randy." He looked to be standing on a street within some type of suburban development. It wasn't clear whether he was trying to appear tough or heroic or scary or even—and I'm reaching here—wise.

I thought: *So who the fuck is Randy S.? Is he well known in the D.C. area? A politician? A famous lobbyist? A local celebrity?*

And who exactly is Noah B., who wrote and "typed" this?

The original price of the book was $8.99 but it was being resold at the garage sale for twenty-five cents. I paid with one dollar and told the now former owner to keep the change. I'm generous like that.

Back at my parents' house, in my old childhood bedroom, in which to stay can be a surreal experience in the best of circumstances, downright hallucinogenic at others, I read the book in full. When I finished (after two, three hours at the most), I immediately returned to the very beginning—and began again.

I had never read anything quite like this work of . . . *what?*

It was a biography of a local thirty-something named Randy S. He worked at various retail gigs and odd occupations before he came into money. He liked women a whole lot. He had, let's just say, pedestrian tastes when it came to TV shows and books and music.

Randy had many ideas for creative projects that he hoped to one day get off the ground.

For instance, he had an idea for a "clean yet efficient" device to kill insects. The invention would be called an "Insuck-Ta-Side," a vacuum-type appliance used for sucking up bugs. The insects could then be humanely discharged back into the wild. Simple. Safe. "Girls will love it."

Another idea: flavored sex lubricant. Suggested flavors would include barbecue, peppermint, hot spice, Tropical Breeze, and Chocolatini.

This way, women, too, "can enjoy the process."

Randy's favorite method of relaxing was to sit in his big fluffy recliner and just "chill" in front of the big screen. The recliner had five pockets for remotes. Also, a cup holder big enough for a Big Gulp.

And a vibrating foot massage.

Randy was a self-described "outside the box" thinker. He loved hitting Ocean City, Maryland on summer weekends and even, on occasion, winter weekends, when there was less "riff raff." His favorite Baldwin was William because he wasn't as "puffy" as the rest. He didn't like Michael Jackson but he did adore Aerosmith (but only the *mid-career years*).

In Randy's opinion, the U2 musical *Spider-Man: Turn Off the Dark* was "unbelievably underrated." So was the little-known Huey Lewis and the News' 2001 album *Plan B*.

As were "clean and odorless" women.

As were "deaf women."

So there was that. But was there anything else to Randy? Had he accomplished anything of any worth?

Not really.

But . . . well, here's one thing:

Randy's grandmother, whom he called his "Mam-Mam," died five years before this book was originally published in January 2016.

Mam-Mam was not a rich woman but she did own a considerable plot of land outside D.C. with a non-working farm and a 19th century house in which generations were raised, including Mam-Mam and Randy.

The entirety of Mam-Mam's will was left to Randy after she died of a heart attack in February 2011, including the large plot of land that Randy promptly sold to a suburban developer for a tidy sum ("more than seven figures, less than eight, but still enough to strut").

So what did Randy do with this newfound windfall? Did he purchase a new home?

Well, yes. He purchased a brand-new, $950,000 six-bedroom town home that sat at the top of a hill overlooking his former farm, which no longer contained Mam-Mam's old house. It had been torn down.

Did Randy purchase a new car to replace his 1989 Pontiac Grand Am?

Why, yes. A 2013 Hummer H3 with "RNDY82" vanity plates.

Randy's most important decision—at least as far as we're concerned—was hiring a writer (the aforementioned Noah B.) to move into his brand-new town home and live with him for one year in order to pen his life story. While Randy is a "brilliant" writer, he has dyslexia and words tend to get all "a-scrumbled." Also, he never "quite learned to type" and he wasn't about to start now.

Noah, the typist of this book, was a recent graduate of the University of Maryland, with a degree in literature. Struggling to make it as a poet and fiction writer after moving back home, he noticed an ad Randy had placed in *The Washington City Paper*.

Noah figured he'd take on the interesting—if somewhat unorthodox—gig until he found his sea legs. Beats working as a waiter or in the retail world, right?

I was taken aback by it all. The book I had stumbled upon was a modern-day version of a 15th century biography commissioned by a wealthy Medici patron, flattering and complimentary and prone to purple prose, but with more references to flat-screen televisions and the Bloomin' Onions at the Gaithersburg, Maryland Outback.

This book that you now hold in your hands is an honest and fascinating (and very suburban) take on a very individual character. If this memoir were to somehow wind up buried and discovered centuries from now—perhaps beneath Randy's extensive paper-towel collection—a future reader could seemingly do a whole lot worse than to take a dip into this skewed, steaming pot of 21st century American political, social and pop-cultural gumbo. (That is, of course, if a future reader were to ever understand Randy's very unique coinages for women's anatomy.)

Although Randy's online thumbprint isn't huge, I did manage to locate him within a few days. It wasn't the toughest of assignments: Randy was still living in the same suburban development and town home that's described within.

Randy was very happy with me reaching out. Confused but thrilled: *How did you find the book? Only 300 copies were printed! Why do you want to re-publish it? Will all proceeds go to me? Will I now become famous?*

So much for my original theory that this book was a work of Nabokovian pretentions. There was no irony intended.

Yes, I assured Randy: beyond the printing costs, all proceeds would, indeed, revert back to him. I had found the book at a garage sale in Poolesville. I don't know how the owners had originally found his book or why they'd ever want to part with it. I wanted to re-publish his biography under my own imprint; I found it fascinating and thought that other readers would, too. I wasn't making fun of it. I truly found it incredible. Offensive at times, but incredible.

On the other hand, no, he would most likely not become famous. Sorry about that. Or maybe he would. Who knows?

Negotiations lasted just a few days. Our only major disagreement seemed to hinge on whether or not to publish Randy's full name. He very much encouraged me to do so. He wanted to get "laid, spelunking in paddy pelt." Why else would he and Noah spend a year writing a book? "C'mon, dude! Please! I *mean* it!" Randy was only half kidding. Or maybe more than half. It was difficult to tell.

We came to an agreement. Randy's last name wouldn't be used. We live in a litigious culture. *Something* in this book was bound to offend *someone*, especially those who reside in either the same development as Randy or live in the same town. I'm a freelance writer. I can barely stay afloat when all is going well, let alone when defending myself (or Randy) from incoming and ongoing litigation.

But here was my concession: if Randy wanted to announce his last name in the press *after* the book was published that would entirely be up to him.

As for Noah—whom I talked with for three hours over the course of a few calls—he's still pursuing his dream of becoming a published fiction writer and poet. He's still living with Randy:

"It's a comfortable situation, one that I'm not entirely happy with, but it'll have to do, at least for the moment. No one's hiring writers. And my dream book—a novel about a twenty-something American in Madrid going through a spiritual crisis—doesn't look as if it's going to be finished any time soon! At least until I visit Spain! As for this book, my job was to chronicle Randy's life. That's what I signed on for. That's what I was paid for. To be his loyal 'retainer.' I really hope I did him justice. And I will say this about him: He's a *captivating* piece of work!"

So here's the book.

Would I ever want to move in and become roommates with Randy? Truthfully, no. (Sorry, Randy.)

But to read about him and his life from a good, safe distance, well . . . there are worse activities.

How's that for an endorsement?

I'm confident and hopeful that there will be future Randy biographies down the road. He's still so young, only in his thirties! He and Noah could pop out additional volumes every few years—and could do so easily!

It would be the modern-day version of the diaries of Samuel Pepys . . . if Pepys partied his ass off at Club Seacrets in Ocean City, Maryland.

Another note: I have not changed one word from the original version, beyond abbreviating last names. The design is also exactly the same. It's a self-published book. It doesn't look or read great. If it's quality or high-end design you're after, look elsewhere.

The only differences—the only major differences—are the addition of this introduction, and the lack of a spiral binding. What you hold in your hands is *exactly* what I found at the garage sale.

As they say, "it is what it is."

I hope you enjoy.

Mike Sacks

Chapter One: BEGINNINGS

Randy S._____ steps from out of his luxurious town home and onto the second-floor backyard balcony overlooking I-270. The morning traffic heading east from Frederick into Washington has slowed to a crawl.

Randy takes a sip from his favorite "LET'S DO THIS!" mug, filled with steaming instant coffee, with just a hint of Vanilla Yoo-hoo. Steam escapes into the cold mid-January air. This man is thirty-four years old but looks no older than twenty-one. He is endowed with an imposing physical brawn as well as an impressive intellect. He takes a deep breath. His voice is most pleasant to find oneself listening to: melodious.

"I hate a few things in life," Randy starts. "Not many. But a few. Guy librarians. Homeless people with attitude. Movies that end with a twist. Black and white movies. Obviously, *The Wizard of Oz* sucks. I just have no patience for it. I hate the manager at the Baskin-Robbins on Rockville Pike. I despise him. He minimizes the number of pink-spoon samples. For him it's five. I need at least 10. But this was before they delivered, so that changed some things."

Randy pauses. And then continues:

"Time to backtrack. My Mam-Mam raised me. My father is dead. Everyone hated my dad. That's what people say. Supposedly he had tattoos on his balls. One read 'Sweet,' the other 'Sour.' He died onstage at the Frederick Bluegrass Fest, karaoking 'The Ballad of Jed Clampett'. He was jammed up off the reds. It wasn't even his turn to sing. With two you get egg roll, right? Cry me a sad one.

"As far as my mother, she ran off to breed another family in California when I was six. She saw the movie *Hair* on Cinemax and got the hippy dippy dreams in her spacy head. She met a deaf plumber, Chuck, who owned a motorcycle. I met him once. Chuck gave me a high-five. He taught me how to deaf-sign to Bon Jovi's 'Livin' On a Prayer.' I still remember. A good bar trick.

"My mother's life was always a rollercoaster. Some real loopydi-loops. Some real intense twists and turns. Sometimes I refer to her as *Gland*-y. Her woman glands always seem to be in overdrive. Her real name is Gladys. She's a dizzy, daffy dame. *All aboard the S.S. Female! Looks to be choppy waters ahead!* Best of luck to her. That choo-choo definitely don't stop at Normalville. Has she written her autobiography at the age of thirty-four? I think not. But the world can thank her for giving birth to the Dandy Randy!"

Randy sighs and blows into his cold hands. "I don't know where I get my smarts, my genius. In some ways, I'm just like every-one else, normal. In other ways, I'm not. A serious dichotomy."

Randy's "LET'S DO THIS!" coffee mug is now empty. He takes one last glance at the cars on their way to work on I-270. It's a steely glance that hides a million stories.

"You know," he says casually, "after I die, which I can't see happening for a super fucking long time, but after I die, if I'd want to be remembered for anything, it'd be for giving great hugs. Also, for being incredibly rich and having a gigantic fucking cock."

Randy laughs heartily and then flips "the bird" to the cars—*suckers!*—and retreats back into his deliciously warm town home.

There's a lot to do. The day is just getting started.

Chapter Two: THE TRUTH

There are quite a few urban legends surrounding Randy and his exceptional, *sui generis* life.

Here is but one: immediately after he was born, Randy took his first walking steps. Not after a few months. Or even a few days. *Immediately*. The doctors and nurses had never witnessed anything quite like this. The national press was notified. Randy became the most famous one-hour-old in the world.

This isn't true. In reality, it took Randy a mere thirteen months to get up on his feet and walk, and then even *less* time to start tearing his way through life.

Another urban legend involving Randy has to do with him making love to over 25,000 women. This is also not true. He's slept with exactly 46 women, all carefully notated and rated in his "Fuck Journal," the lined Mead with the Yosemite Sam sticker on the cover, both guns blazing. It sits next to his "Fart Journal."

The two journals are displayed on the Dekon 2 Tonelli glass coffee table that sits proudly in Randy's spacious living room.

Randy has consummated sexual relations to completion 2,457 times, in three states: Maryland, Virginia and Florida. Of these actions, he would rank 1,264 as "five," meaning the very best. Of these actions, he would only rank thirteen events as a "one," meaning the very worst. And not one of these *ones* is necessarily Randy's fault. "Mostly just girls with an inferiority complex around someone they definitely find more attractive. Intimidation factor. They freeze up."

Sadly, there also exist a few legends that are of the less impressive sort, specifically those that involve Randy and his various run-ins with Maryland state police departments.

Let it be known that Randy has the *greatest* respect for the police and for the dangerous work these brave civil servants perform on a daily and nightly basis. Randy imagines that it must be quite difficult to put your life on the line for the protection of one's community, especially for so very little money. In fact, Randy considers himself really good Facebook friends with a former police officer he's known since the fifth grade. The policeman's name is Alan P._____.

As children, Randy and Alan would light ping-pong balls on fire and watch as the orange-black flames licked the sky. Years later, Alan was arrested for lighting the woods on fire in Cabin John Park in order to impress a waitress at the China Gourmet Bistro in Cabin John Mall. She was not impressed. Five people died. Alan P._____ is no longer a policeman.

As for Randy's arrests . . .

In a story that has been widely reported in the local press, but reported *incorrectly*, Randy was involved in a March 2009 altercation outside a senior citizen center in Rockville.

Randy patiently explains: "It was just a big mix-up. This was when I was younger and much more stupid. I was drunk off cheap wine and had just eaten a huge meal at Bob's Big Boy. My stomach went off kilter. I was on my way home but knew I'd never make it. It's like a World War II pilot who's unable to return to base safely. I don't want to sound like a hero but I was past the PNR. That means 'point of no return.' So I ditched. An elderly is looking out his window and sees me below. He was on the first floor. I was squatting like a mother. Of all the luck. He calls the cops. I was out the next day. Ironically, this asshole was a World War II vet. But he was never a pilot."

Randy tells me this fascinating story while driving his 2013 Hummer H3 to Absolute Electronix on Redland Road in order to have a remote-start system installed. Randy despises the cold Maryland mornings and would much prefer to start his vehicle from *inside* his luxury town home.

"I love all types of music," declares Randy, suddenly and without prompting.

The rock music in the Hummer is blasting something ferocious!

"Anything *good*. I don't care what it is, as long as it's not alternative or punk or edgy or bluegrass or country or classical or reggae or any of that shit. I hate island culture. I like *melody*. My biggest musical influence is probably the 1980s super group Asia. They released only two albums but they're both insanely amazing. Loved

Asia since I was a damned kid! Strange name—as far as I can tell, not one person in it is from China. I also love Jefferson Starship. 'We Built This City.' They built it on rock and roll. How cool is that?"

Randy pauses. "Listen." He flicks on his Pioneer Stage 4 DEX-P99RS, and the lush sounds of "Heat of the Moment" blasts through the $124 Alpine Direct Fit PSS-31GM speakers.

"YOU CAN TRULY HEAR THE QUALITY IN THE MELODY AND IN THE LYRICS!" Randy screams over the delightful, synthy music. "IT'S ALL IN THERE! YOU JUST GOT TO BE LIKE AN EXCAVATOR AND HEAR IT! AND I CAN HEAR IT! I LOVE ASIA!"

The music is turned down to a lower volume. Randy's voice returns to its regular, pleasant level. "I can't scream. It ruins my vocal cords. Okay. This is hard to talk about. But I do want this in the book. And I have to be completely up front. People can always see through bullshit." He pauses. He glances out the driver's window.

What he's about to say won't be easy for him to talk about . . . and yet he bravely pushes forward regardless:

"Okay. So. I *have* played ball with the law. To me, it's a game. Like a kitty cat teasing a barn critter. I admit it. I find it fun."

Phew. It's out there. Randy visibly breathes easier. A great weight has been lifted off his broad, muscular shoulders. "I do want to get out the *truth*. Not the crap the *Potomac Almanac* keeps reporting. That's one of the reasons for this memoir. Among *many*."

The traffic is snarled on Rockville Pike. We have at least twenty minutes until we arrive at Absolute Electronix. Randy turns off Asia and switches over to his favorite radio program, *The Sports Junkies*, on 106.7 FM. The boys are talking in a funny way about how the Washington Wizards never seem capable of pulling off a vital win in the playoffs: "The Wizards ain't nothin' but a batch of dribbling doofuses!" The Junkies laugh. Randy is barely listening. He is full-on concentrating on what he's about to say. When he gets to it, it comes out in a beautiful torrent:

"It's June 2010. I'm working at the Pen Boutique in Montgomery Mall. I've risen to the rank of assistant manager. I sell exotic pens, desk accessories, leather business items. The job's okay. At least I'm inside, with air conditioning. Auntie Anne's is across the way, which I love. Mini pretzel dogs. *Whoof!*"

Randy, without notice, breaks into an extremely funny and very loud barking spree. It lasts for more than one minute.

"So when I'm not waiting on customers," Randy continues after done barking, "I'm writing songs. Jotting down ideas. I have a *million* of 'em! It's flat-out bananas! Crank it and spank it!"

Among his many, many creative talents, Randy is an established songwriter, with more than 200 songs to his credit, six of which have been recorded by Randy himself on GarageBand and available for immediate download by request at Numberonelover453@yahoo.com for a very reasonable $1.99 each, payable by personalized check and then mailed to PO Box 237, Poolesville, Maryland, 20837.

Randy also maintains a very popular Twitter feed, under the name *RandyIsDaMan*, with more than 25,000 followers. In comparison, the Salvation Army has a mere 15,000 followers.

"I'm a brilliant writer but I did grow up with dyslexia. Words get all a-scrumbled and a-bumbled. I'll admit to that. A customer comes into the Pen Boutique one day with a sick kid. Bald head. The kid has cancer but is getting better. I'm happy to hear that. I rub his head for good luck, which he loves. His mother is buying a pen to write thank-you notes to all those who visited in the hospital. I ask the kid about his stay. He says, 'The food sucked.' I tell him I disagree. *Vehemently*. I *love* hospital food. I eat at the Shady Grove Hospital cafeteria all the damn time! There's a ton of Jamaican cooks who make kick-ass beef patties. That's the *only* aspect of island culture I like. No one ever asks what I'm doing there. Sometimes I wear one of those mirrors on a band around my head. Maybe they think I'm a world-famous surgeon. Name it and claim it. Blab it and grab it, you know?

"I say to the kid, 'Wasn't there *one thing* you liked about living in the hospital? *Anything*?' He tells me that yes, there was. Musicians. Clowns. Jugglers. Performers who do it for free.

"This gives me an idea. I show up at Shady Grove with a guitar. This is the next day. The nurse at the entrance asks what I'm doing there. I tell her I'm performing for the sick kids. What I don't tell her is that I've been trying to do a lot more live performing but haven't had much luck booking gigs. So the hospital is perfect! Talk about a receptive audience! I ask her, 'Where is the cancer for kids section?' She tells me that it's on the fourth floor, and I go on up.

"I don't wait for permission. Randy Dandy don't wait for nothin'. I just start strumming that guitar. Kids start gathering. Even the nurses stop to watch. I bounce into a kid's room and bang into a new song I wrote called 'Life is Funny.' It's about a mouse who lives in the pocket of a kid's T-shirt. The kid is about to die in the Holocaust. It's based on that movie about the super cool dad pretending that both him and his son aren't in a concentration camp. It's all a big game. I fucking *love* that movie. I think it's the best Holocaust movie ever made!

"In my song, the kid dies. I go to another room and crank out a blues song—think early George Thorogood. It's about how you can't always hook up with the hotty you think you can when you're young. Right? There's a lot of irony in that song. And truth. And sadness. The kid really looks like he's enjoying it. Clapping. Trying to. It's hard with the needles.

"When I get to the third room, the cops arrive. This kid's asleep anyway. See, this is what frustrates me and what the papers never get right. I was not *playing* the guitar. I was only *pretending* to. I don't *know* how to play the guitar. The guitar was the blow-up kind. Plastic. You see them at weddings and kids' parties. So that was incorrect. Also, my songs are not dirty. They are *realistic*. They are for music lovers of *all ages*. Excuse me for playing the blues and for not feeding burn victims Jell-O squares! I'm being sarcastic."

Back in the present, Randy beeps his horn and shouts at the driver to his left to move the "fuck over" so he can make his way into the left lane. "You know, if I had to do it all over again, I'd ask permission to sing first. Maybe play songs that weren't so bluesy and depressing. Something poppier and more upbeat. Less about death. Less about selling your soul to the devil. Less about wanting puss, I guess."

Randy lights a cigarette and rolls down his window. The traffic is particularly bad today. But this doesn't seem to affect Randy. Like most successful and affluent citizens, he has few pressing obligations.

"Okay, so when I was arrested again, in 2013, I'm no longer working at the Pen Boutique in Montgomery Mall. I was fired because I had too many suggestions. And because I was eight-balling a chick behind the knife counter. She worked at Forever 21. More like

Forever *45*, if you know what I mean. Then I went to work selling big screens at the Big Screen Store in Rockville. *Big-ass* TVs."

Randy taps the wheel of his Hummer. "Here's the thing about me. I hate imperfection. Physically. It depresses me. A bigger bunch of toads you'll never find than the ones I worked with at Big Screen. *Really* ugly. Like ancient hairy people you see living in the woods on the History channel. But there was one that I got along with great. His name was Goose. *Goose!* He loved strippers! He's really the main instigator who got me into all this here trouble. Truly! It's Goose's fault!

"Goose shows me a picture of an escort he knows by the name of April. Mid-twenties, nice blond hair. A substantial pair of Darwin's Dinglers. I *have* to meet her. I email her and she writes back. She seems interested but only because that's her job. It's very easy for me to tell. Some people are able to 'read' other people better than others. I'm a good people 'reader.' Everyone has a 'tell.' Her particular 'tell' was that she said she wanted to 'fuck' for 'money.'

"*Fine.* So I throw her a surprise. I ask her to go see a movie with me. She's definitely not expecting this one, right? She recommends *12 Years a Slave.* I say yes even though I never heard of it. She tells me what it's about. I'm thinking it must have a kick-ass rap soundtrack. I love rap. My favorite rap group is 3rd Bass. Two white guys. One used a cane but he could actually walk just fine. It was just a prop! *Brilliant.*

"I was wrong about the movie. Not a second of rap. It's four hours of guys running through fields. The soundtrack sucks. I turn to April and say, 'Let's hit Dave & Busters.' She smiles. I *have* her. The D&Bs on Colesville Road in Silver Spring is the very best. The burgers are truly legendary. All the managers know that I don't like my buns wet. I like 'em toasted and on the side, not touching the meat or the goddamn pickle. *Full-metal burger.*

"April and I walk into D&Bs like we own the place. The manager on duty that night, Ken, nods. That's all it takes. I'm like a family member. He knows the routine. Past the bar, past the bathrooms, into the far-right corner, my chair facing out.

"I never play the video games at D&Bs, for a number of reasons. One, a lot of Chinese kids always are hogging my favorite games. Two, I hate touching the joysticks *before* I eat. Guess what?

I then have to wash my hands incredibly well again. Three, I have an addictive personality. Once I start, it's pretty much impossible to stop. And I'm competitive! It's like my paper towel collection from rest stops. A few years back, I took one piece home from a rest stop on my way back from King's Dominion. Then I brought home a few more. Before you know it, thousands are hanging all over my bedroom. It's the biggest collection in all of southern Maryland. They're all different. Each one. They're like the wood trolls Mam-Mam used to collect. Wood only. She hated plastic. There's one guy in Baltimore who has more paper towels but that's fucking Baltimore.

"April and I still go to the movies, every other Sunday. Sexually, April is the very, very best. She's H.A.S.B.Y. *Hot as shit in bed, yo!* She knows what to touch and what not to touch when daddy needs milked. So much easier than a normal girlfriend or wife! And I can have fun with her. She lets me twist her nipples as if I'm drawing an Etch A Sketch. She knows when to talk and when to shut her yapper. She understands, at times, I can get lazy. And when that happens, she doesn't grow upset. She only knows it's time to take care of herself. A woman's privates remind me of a Shar Pei puppy. A ton of folds surrounded by a ton of fur. Confusing. She also knows that I have to listen to The Sports Junkies whenever we're doing it. I like to multi-task and I think sex should be fun. If I laugh out loud, that should be fun, too. Or even a chuckle. She's free to chuckle herself. I'm fine with all that!

"On December 1, 2013, April and I are at D&Bs. This has all been well reported. Like I said, we saw *12 Years a Slave* and it sucked. But for some reason it gets us super bang-bang horny."

Randy grows quiet. It's a story that has been widely reported on the local TV news and elsewhere, but, as is typical, it was reported *incorrectly*. It is now Randy's turn to tell the story as it *truly* happened.

Randy good-naturedly explains: "It was just a big mix-up. I was drunk off at least fifteen Razzleberry Smashtails. Maybe more. My head wasn't screwed up right. The press made it sound as if we were going at it like two feral monkeys in the woods. *Not true.*

"But there were two problems. One, we used the handicapped stall in the women's room. Just our luck that a handicapped *woman* was at D&Bs that night. How often does this happen? Fucking *never.*

Handicapped *men*? Sure. All the goddamn time.

"Two, my Ipod was playing REM's 'Everybody Hurts,' which depressed the hell out of everyone in that bathroom. The handicapped chick complained the loudest. Like she doesn't have *enough* to fucking worry about!"

We're now pulling into the parking lot of Absolute Electronix on Redland Road. The lot is empty and Randy manages to quickly find a space.

He always does.

"Third, April is *that* loud. But that's her job, right? You'd think people would understand that! What's she being paid $250 an hour for? To quietly play fucking Parcheesi?!"

Randy is now exiting his Hummer, striding purposely towards the store. As he enters, he laughs. "She has to earn her money, right? And it's not like I pay her any *less* to sit through movies! Same damn fee. So she really gives it her all when we're scrumping."

And then, quietly: "Anyway, it's all Goose's fault."

"Randy!" screams an Absolute Electronix employee. "What up, boy?!"

"My wallet is hotter than a backyard smoker and I'm burnin' to buy!" retorts Randy.

The employee laughs very, very hard. It is extremely funny.

Sometimes it seems as if e*veryone* in Montgomery County Maryland knows and enjoys Randy S._____.

And Randy is *a-okay* with that.

Hooray for Randy!

"Randy-Isms"

"Never trust a dude who points with his pinkie"

"The more talented the drummer, the less reliance on his drumstick twirling"

"If you are a retarded character in a film, you're a whole lot less annoying if you're from the South"

"Any song with a tambourine sucks"

"Mustaches only look cool on dwarves and midgets"

"Urinating your name in the snow is acceptable. Shitting it is not."

"Trust me: No good can come from hot-tubbing after sunrise!"

"Never be the one to start or finish a stadium wave"

"The fatter the friend, the more they will lecture you on dietary advice"

"*Anything* goes better with Old Bay. Even *that*."

"There ain't no cool way to eat a popsicle."

"Only chicks in musicals enjoy kissing in the rain."

"Flavored dental floss should never be sweeter than the *foods you want to get rid of.*"

"Flying superheroes get laid the most. Superheroes who swim, the least."

"Only assholes valet park at the mall"

"Any movie is better with a hot-air balloon or a talking chimp"

"Always remove the bar-code from store-bought flowers"

"Never allow your fashion sense to be dictated by 'island' culture"

"The fourth season of *Crank Yankers* was the worst"

"If you bring a mitt to a baseball game, you're an idiot. Only drunks and Yankee fans catch foul balls."

"The more fancy a man's signature, the more he's hiding"

"Cordless phones always disappoint eventually"

"Libraries are basically homeless shelters"

"Avoid any stripper named after a domestic car"

"Ketchup is for losers. Mustard, winners."

"I don't care if you're in a wheelchair. If you're an asshole, you're just an asshole in a wheelchair."

Chapter Three: COMIC-STRIPS

"I adore humor," says Randy, soaking in his oversized fiber-glass gelcoat bathtub, within his gorgeous 400 square-foot faux-marbled bathroom. "I can safely say that my humor IQ is in the genius range."

The lights are off and Randy is "dark jamming," his term for submerging himself up to his neck in warm bath water and allowing his thoughts to trek wherever they might desire. "Like a sensory deprivation tank but cheaper. Right now I'm just gonna talk. Anything can come out. Be *prepared*."

Today's topic is syndicated comic-strips, an art form Randy grew up with and still very much enjoys each morning in *The Washington Post*.

"I've always dreamed of writing and drawing a hugely popular comic-strip. *I love comics!* Not the fake superhero crap. *Funny ones!* If I had to list my favorites, they'd be *Zits, Funky Winkerbean, Snuffy Smith, Momma*. Momma reminds me of Mam-Mam. Just the way she looks. And her attitude. Oh, and I fucking love *Andy Capp*!

"They don't make comics like *Andy Capp* anymore. They can't. Wouldn't be allowed. The *Post* got rid of it. It's about *real* life. It's about how a man struggles with being married. I've been married twice. I can tell you that it's spot on. *Andy Capp* is an *extremely* realistic look at marriage and dealing with difficult women. Mrs. Capp is always raising her rolling pin but Andy is way too much a man to stand for it. He'll just turn around and head back to the bar.

"My first marriage was to the daughter of the owner of a TCBY on Rockville Pike. I used to call the place *Totally Crummy Bitch of a Yob*. I worked there for two years when I was twenty-eight to thirty. I clawed my way up to assistant manager. It wasn't easy. But I did it.

"How do I put this delicately? I'm trying to be super dignified about this. Sara was fucking crazy. Off her lally-looper! Somewhere over the brainbow! Elevator never reaching the stars!

"She had real mental issues and we didn't connect. She came to believe that I had planted a bug in her brain. I only *claimed* that

I had planted a bug in her brain. It's not like I would know how to technically do that! I wouldn't call Radio Shack and ask, *'Hey! I'm looking to implant a bug in my wife's brain! Can you help? What type of battery should I use? Double or triple A?'* I had the marriage annulled after a few weeks. She was nice. She now owns an Edible Arrangements. We're still great Facebook friends but, to be honest, she was never on my creative wavelength. I'll give you an example.

"I love zombies. One of my better comic-strip ideas is to draw a family of Zombies called The Zombanskies. They're Zombies but also a typical suburban family. Sara thought the idea was stupid. She didn't want me to spend our $25,000 on hats, T-shirts, dolls. She wanted the money for her mental hospital stays. I tried to explain to her—and I'd do it over and over again—why it was absolutely necessary to have this stuff in order to sell the idea to a newspaper syndicate. But she wouldn't listen. Stubborn as all get out! I had another amazing comic idea called *Millennial Blues*. It's like *Cathy* but for Millennials. There's Benny. He's twenty-six. The partier of the bunch. He's a struggling rock musician. Writes a lot of cool lyrics about getting hum-hums in the back booth of a KFC . . ."

Randy stops talking and practically slaps his forehead. "Whoa! I just had another idea for a syndicated comic. It just came to me! I would absolutely love to do a strip on Ayn Rand's writings. I *love* her. I've never read any of her books but I do love her. I agree on a lot. Can you write that down? My hands are wet. Yeah, that could work. I also love Dean Koontz. I own all his books. They're in alphabetical order in my living room. What else? Maybe something about Jim Jones. I'm fascinated by that guy's story. All that *power*."

Randy politely asks his listener to make the bath water a tad warmer. After it reaches the specified temperature conducive to his creativity, Randy continues: "My second wife, Denise, was nice enough but the union didn't last long at all. We parted on very good terms, although she did end up getting half of my Redskins collectible cards. That sucks. But we're still incredible Facebook friends. I have a lot of *amazing* Facebook friends. Except for that asshole manager at Baskin-Robbins. I blocked him.

"Do you want to know how Denise and I met? I was training to be a Navy SEAL. I've always loved those guys—*oh, that's another comic-strip idea! That would be awesome!* Team SEAL Six! I'll have to ask the government. I've always wanted to be a SEAL! Ever since *G.I. Jane*. I fucking love that movie! When I was still living on Mam-Mam's farm, I built a replica of a SEAL training course and I'd post Facebook photos of me training. Denise saw the photos and got real excited. We started talking. On our second date, she gave me a 'swish and a wish,' which is when a girl gives you a hummer inside a car wash. We got married the next day."

Randy sighs loudly. "I really wanted that marriage to work! I really and truly did. But Denise wasn't into historical role play. I like to pretend I'm a 17th century detective hunting down Jack the Ripper. Like, 'Excuse me, I am looking for Jack the Ripper and I do wonder if thee might be of any assistance?' But I say it in a British accent. I then proceed to ask if I can have sex with the prostitute. She's saucy and always says yes. I've found this to be catnip for the kitty cats. Not Denise.

"She also gave me zero support. Like when I wanted calf implants, something I've always wanted. Both of my legs have always been way too thin. To be fair, we were low on dough. She wanted to give all our money to her mother for some type of medical treatment for cancer. I soon quit her and began dating an indoor lacrosse cheerleader, Alexa. That lasted a week. She was crispy but didn't have the mental goods. Denise's mom died."

Randy points to his head.

"God, I have so many ideas. I wrote a porn version of *Groundhog Day* called *Horndog Day*. The character gets laid every goddamn day but in a different way! It's hilarious. And sexy has hell. It *will* get made and soon!

"To get back to *Millennial Blues*, there's the character of Benny, who I've already mentioned, and then there's Stuey, who's twenty-eight. He's the nerd of the group. Loves to read long novels. I can't think of any at the moment. But they're long. There's Becca, twenty-one. Major-league hotty. Stuey has a crush and tries to impress her with his amazing yo-yo tricks. The Captain is thirty-one. Older than the rest. Been around the block. He once got drunk and shaved off all his body hair and then ran into a seafood restaurant. I did this once."

Randy makes a "hurry up" motion. "My brain is in overdrive now. I've reached cruising altitude. Or *attitude*. Ha! Have you ever fantasized about having an alien pet? That could make for a cool comic. He'd make my bed. And cook me frozen waffles by just point-ing a finger at 'em. And if it was a girl alien, she'd give me a morning yank. I'd tell her, 'Wake me up at a quarter to spank.' And the alien's name would be Maggi. Slang it and bang it!

"Okay, I'm done for now," declares Randy, standing and motioning to his favorite thirsty towel. He purchased it for $4.99 at a Mobile on Rockville Pike. It features a woman in a bikini giving the finger. It's incredibly humorous.

"I can't overwork it or I get migraines. Even the most power-ful computers are capable of overheating." Handed the towel, Randy steps from out of the tub and makes his way over to the mirror, misty with condensation. Randy bought this very special gift for himself a few years back on the boardwalk of Ocean City, Maryland.

He rubs at the mirror until his image becomes clear. Engraved at the bottom, in gold-lettering and in cursive, is the following in-scription:

Coolest Guy in the World!

Watching Randy impishly wink at his own reflection, it would be impossible to argue.

Randy's Favorite 64 Movies

White Chicks
("seen it a million times. Fucking hilarious!")

The Golden Child

Jack and Jill
("Adam Sandler always makes me laugh.
He made April laugh, too. I miss her.")

Mr. Holland's Opus
("the kid was deaf but sweet as fuck")

Drive

Heaven is for Real
("it is. I've been there.")

Drillbit Taylor

Who Framed Roger Rabbit

Buster

Walk Like a Man
("Howie Mandel is raised by wolves or something")

Last Tango in Paris
("you got to have the sound off")

Year One

Superbad
("I love anything Judd Apatow does!")

Judge Dredd
("Stallone only")

Zookeeper

The Sitter

Pirates of the Caribbean:
On Stranger Tides

Cowboys and Aliens

Arthur
("The new one. I can't understand the European one.")

Norbit

Daddy Day Camp

The Number 23
("This picture will blow your mind. 23 is now my favorite number.")

Napoleon Dynamite
("I know every line except for the romance stuff.")

Dodgeball

Nacho Libre

The Cobbler
("This movie made me cry")

Ted 2

Entourage
("The fucking best")

Hook

Baby Geniuses
("the special effects are outrageous")

Universal Soldier: The Return

Chill Factor

Dream a Little Dream

Communion
("It's all true. God, how I would love to be picked up by aliens and taken to another planet. I'd be real popular.")

The Karate Kid Part III
("the best of the bunch. Ralph Macchio was forty-seven when he shot this one")

The Adventures of Ford Fairlane

Dice Rules
("the most hilarious live stand-up concert ever caught on film")

Slappy and the Stinkers

I Still Don't Know What I Did Last Summer

A Night at the Roxbury
("this never shows up on any best-of lists but it's so fucking good. You can't ask for more in a comedy than this one.")

Chairman of the Board
("I laughed so hard I pissed into the lap of the guy sitting next to me. This was at home. Just joking. Not about the pissing.")

Rock Dog

Hardly Working

The Emoji Movie
("the critics blasted it but it's really subversively brilliant. I hate critics.")

Alice Through the Looking Glass
("trippy")

Zoolander 2
("even funnier than the first")

Gods of Egypt

Dirty Grandpa
("when the fake grandpa takes a real dump on a high-dive
at a public pool, I cried I laughed so hard")

Scary Movie 5

Life is Beautiful
("the best Holocaust movie ever made")

Bucky Larson: Born to Be a Star
("Pauly Shore is the best. Where did he go?")

Atlas Shrugged III:
Who is John Galt?

Nobody's Perfekt

Jesus Christ Superstar
("Mam-Mam's favorite. I loved it except for the goofy hats
on the soldiers. And the music.")

Haunted Honeymoon

Faces of Death II
("real people dying years before the invention of the
internet, incredibly cool!")

Carbon Copy
("Way ahead of its time when it comes
to talking about race issues")

The Slugger's Wife

Fraternity Vacation

The Jar Jar Star Wars. The best one of them all.

Summer Rental

Corky Romano

Black Knight

Scary Movie 2

The Three Stooges
("The new ones, not the dopey old ones")

Home Alone 2
("obviously!")

Chapter Four: INVENTIONS

Randy despises traveling, especially into the city of Washington, and will only do so for one good reason: to file and register hand-drawn copyright blueprints at the U.S. Copyright Office on Independence Avenue. While it is possible to do so remotely, Randy much prefers to do so in person, as his ideas are extremely important to both him and, potentially, to the world.

"I don't like D.C.," says Randy, standing in line at the Copyright Office, registration forms in hand. "There are too many surprises. And not enough culture. I prefer *suburban* culture. But some of my best inventions have come while traveling into the city. Like my SAFE SIT app. Say you're sitting next to a minority on the Metro. You're not so sure they're safe. You take a photo of the guy. *Secretly.* I'd suggest doing so quickly without them noticing. Like you would with a voyeur sex shot. The photo is then automatically uploaded to a national criminal database using facial technology. Then either 'SAFE' or 'DANGEROUS' will come up on the screen. Apple knows all about this. Also the Department of Defense. I'm still waiting to hear back from both. It'll save a lot of lives. It's that simple.

"Another app I invented: WHERE THE SUN DON'T SHINE. Say you're on the Metro or in a car about to take a trip. What side of the car is the sun going to be obnoxiously flashing into? Using GPS and your eventual destination, this'll tell you. The sun is fine but not for more than an hour. Then my psyche hurts.

"I came up with another app called OKCupid PLUS. It's no surprise that most of the women on OKCupid are hideous. I once saw a midget on it. A fucking midget! I love midgets for fun—if they're riding on the shoulders of normal people or in a Van Halen video. *But to date?* Come on. I've seen a fatso with one leg. I guess it's not all bad: she'd only have weighed more with it. *Whistle before you explode so I can get out of the room, right?* This app will plug directly into your OKCupid account and weed out all the uglies, and then contact the hotties and automatically send them a pre-written message: *I saw you on OKCupid. What up girl?! How is your week going? What are you doing? Do you like beer?"*

The line is slow and Randy fidgets. There's just way too much to accomplish today.

"I sent it to OKCupid, but haven't heard back. I wouldn't mind a no, but I would love to hear back. One more app, BAR NONE. You're at a bar. You've run out of things to talk about. You don't have your yo-yo. You've forgotten your magic tricks. You don't know a damn thing about the current political situation. So what do you do? *What do you say?"*

Randy waits for an answer that doesn't arrive.

"You go to BAR NONE and you input information on the Betty you're trying to impress. Age, ethnicity, height, weight, looks. Out pops the *perfect* small-talk suggestion. It's specifically tailored to your situation. 'Are you a C or a double B cup?' Or 'Did you know it wasn't Kool-Aid that Jim Jones used to kill his followers? It was Flavor Aid?' Women *love* that sort of shit!"

The line is moving along now. Ideas are flowing.

"I invented a ton of stuff! Flavored sex lubrication. Isn't that something you kick yourself for not having thought of first? All of the flavors that girls love: Barbecue, peppermint, hot spice, Tropical Breeze, Chocolatini, you name it. This way women can *also* enjoy the process!

"My favorite all-time invention is called the Insuck-Ta-Side. I thought of this when I was killing a praying mantis at Mam-Mam's. All girls are afraid of insects. It's basically a vacuum with a long, thin hose that you aim at ceilings or corners. It'll suck up *anything* you want! But here's the best part: Flip a switch and the insect comes flying out. *They don't have to die.* It's clean yet efficient. Girls will love it. And I *love* girls! *Clean* girls."

A man in line ahead turns around to face Randy, but then quickly turns back around. Randy lowers his voice. The last thing he needs now is for one of his ideas to be stolen, even if they all *are* legally copyrighted.

"Hey! Here's something I am super fucking excited about! A graphic novel about Aerosmith, three hundred pages long. A story based on the lyrics to 'Love in an Elevator,' which is the best. I could have made it *six* hundred pages. I hate their early shit. Sounds like raccoons rutting. Mid-career all the way. Steve Tyler once autographed a baseball for me. I saw him at an O's game. I think it was Steve Tyler. I lost the ball. Even girls are gonna dig this graphic novel and they hate all that cool shit!"

The woman in back of Randy says, "Excuse me?"

Randy nods. "Sorry, I was just talking to my friend." And then, very quietly, "See, that's why I don't get along with most girls. They have very poor senses of humor. Their humor IQ tends to be in the rumdum range. I have to tell you a story: I'm at a party. This was a few years back. I spot a beautiful girl. *Gorgeous.* Just drop-dead. I make my way over. I start the patter. Going strong and stronger. But nothing's working. Even the 'How about a hug, luv?' line bombs. That's from Andy Capp.

"She was one of those girls who are never happy. *Ever.* She walks away, starts gossiping with her bitchy friends. The only thing that works in this sort of situation—any type of situation—is comedy. Or cool small talk. Or magic. Or yo-yo tricks. But mostly comedy.

"So I've done this before. I imitate dogs great. I can do *any* sort of voice for any type of animal or situation. It's just something I've always been good at. But dogs are a specialty. So I drop to my knees and crawl on all fours over to this woman. I'm just oontzing and poontzing my way over. I get behind her and start sniffing. Sniff *sniff!* Sniff *sniff!* She finally turns around. Takes forever! Her friends are startled. But then I really dig deep into this dog character. I ain't headed back now. She asks, 'What *exactly* are you doing?!'"

Randy is laughing very hard. Tears are flowing down his cheeks. Randy can entertain anyone, even himself.

"I'm still in the role, right? So in my best high-pitched doggy-type voice, I say really, *really* loud, so everyone can hear, 'I juss sniffin' yo butt!'

"This was at a 'Mingles with the Singles' party at a church. '*I juss sniffin' yo butt!*' The whole point was that I was communicating as a dog! But she didn't laugh. It reminds me of something . . . I once asked a woman at a party what her 'shaving schedule' was. I was just curious. *Genuinely!* She didn't answer. Stuck up. I wouldn't mind a no, but how about a *something*? Or maybe she was laughing but only inwardly."

Randy appears sad. "There's an exception to anything, I guess. It was just a wiggy goof."

At last, it's Randy's turn. But he's not yet finished with his story: "Wouldn't a dog say that if it could? 'I juss sniffin' yo butt?' *Of course* it would! That's what dogs do! *They sniff butts*! Jesus!"

Randy, now at the head of the line, is asking this question to the bureaucrat sitting behind the desk, who is nodding in agreement.

"Another type who has no sense of humor," mumbles Randy, behind a cupped hand. "Government workers. Being paid on *my* fucking well-earned dime."

And then, back to the woman behind the desk, as nice as can be: "I am here today to file a copyright for an invention of my own invention!"

Randy grandly hands over his appropriately filled-out forms, all written on the back of Fuddrucker paper placemats. A few have on them gravy stains in very interesting patterns.

"It's a lazy-eye patch with the Metallica logo on it," he explains proudly. "It'll help kids who love the band. And who have wobbly eyes. It'll help them make friends. My Mam-Mam made a prototype for me when I was a kid. I still have mine in storage. I'd wear it but it stinks all weird."

Randy makes the thumb's up sign.

For now, the line behind Randy is long. In front of him, however, there exists an amazing future, spread out endlessly, as far as the mind can possibly imagine, straight into eternity.

Go, Randy!

More Cool Randy Inventions

A Van Halen inspired carpal tunnel splint

Mudflaps on a wheelchair that read: "MY OTHER RIDE IS YOUR MOM!"

"Something to do with squeezing oranges and not getting that shit on your hands. I hate oranges."

"Those hospital automatic soap foaming dispensers for the car, especially after touching a toll worker's hand."

A "fleshlight" surrounded with fake, soft hair but not too much hair

A vending machine that dispenses tiny cards with funny jokes on them like U R N ASSHOLE!

A cough lozenge that tastes like deep-dish Pizzeria Uno

Sex gloves

Chapter Five: SPRING BREAK

Randy decides to take a much needed week off.

It's late March, a few weeks after Randy has returned from the "Cryptocurrency Convention" in the Pooks Hill Holiday Inn.

He couldn't afford to buy.

But it's now Spring Break.

Just as he's done every Spring Break for the past twelve years, Randy is heading down to Ft. Myers to party his ass off. It's a tradition.

"I have more damn fun down in that town than I do anywhere else. I hate to travel. *Never* do it. Except into D.C. maybe. But I don't consider this travel. This is F-U-N. That spells *fun*. And it *is*. But it hasn't always been without its stink-ass wrinkles."

Randy is leaning back in his Spirit Air seat, wearing his blow-up neck pillow, munching on a smuggled packet of peanuts.

"Not allowed on the plane," he states, holding up the packet. *"Could be too dangerous for the allergic.* That's a conspiracy theory. There are so many. 9/11 was a conspiracy created by the news organizations to have something to talk about. That's clear. Charlie Sheen talks about this. Michelle Obama has a penis. That is true. I've seen photos and charts. Adam and Eve were both sent to Earth from outer space. Where in the hell *else* would they come from?

"President Kennedy shot himself. I know this for a fact. Princess Diana was killed by Mexican mercenaries. That's true. I don't believe Elvis is alive or any of that shit. I believe he never existed. That was a government creation to take people's minds off war. As for that plane no one's ever found, it's in Greenland. When was the last time anyone said anything good or bad about Greenland? They wanted the world's attention. So they forced it to land. Pathetic. I *hate* those people."

Randy settles in for the two-and-a-half-hour flight. He has his iPhone "Chillin' on a Plane" mixes and his *Uncle John's Bathroom Reading* books and his Word Scrambles to puzzle over. But for now,

Randy is more than content to talk about his past Spring Break adventures.

"I first started going when I was twenty-two. I was at Montgomery College. I quit. The professors were idiots. And I never really had the opportunity to party. One year, I said fuck it. This is when I was working as a temp in Rockville. God, I *hated* that job! Bunch of morons. Just Xeroxed and shit. World Bank. I told them all to fuck off and I quit, but not before I left them a little present. Probably *still* wondering where the smell is coming from!

"So I thought, *Where should I head now?* I read something in *Maxim* about Spring Break, and Ft. Myers sounded real cool. I drove down." He laughs. "I couldn't afford fancy air travel like I can now!

"So I go on down. No place to stay. I checked fliers on light poles. There was a house that was looking for more people to offset costs. I show up. It's a bunch of fraternity types from University of Georgia. That's fine. The house is huge. I party my ass off. I see a triple rainbow. Hooked up with a lot of Bettys. Incredible. Fly a kite for the first time. Played Frisbee for the first time. Flew a kite for the second time. Played drinking games but not alone for a change. I'm still great Facebook friends with a lot of these people!

"We called it the Frog Cave. The house was green like a cave where a frog might live. I've been going back ever since. I'm now in charge of the house. *Der commandant! Yavul!* I rent for the week, others pay me. I've never had trouble finding enough kids.

"Crazy shit has happened. *Insane.* Slept with practically an entire nerd sorority from Tulane in 2008. I have that down in my Fuck Journal. That was easy. God, I *love* it down there. 2010 was the worst year! I suffered a 'break.' I went bazookas. Came to believe that hermit crabs were talking to me. Ran along the beach at night until I was tackled by a lifeguard. This is another reason I hate those fuckers. He was off duty. The crabs were telling me to light the boardwalk on fire. I did as they told me. There were people on the boardwalk laughing, throwing fudge and taffy. They were pouring crab fries on the fire to put it out. Big fucking joke.

"The next year was much better. Ironically, I ended up selling bootleg hermit crabs on the boardwalk and made a shit ton of money. A lot of the crabs died. I sold them as young, but they were old. The kids couldn't have afforded the more expensive ones anyway. Everybody won.

"That was the year I was accused of stealing the Frog Cave's 'Rash Cash.' That's the money—mostly change—that was used for suntan lotion, condoms, things like that. I didn't steal it. I was *borrowing* the money to pay for a henna tattoo. It was the Chinese symbol for 'virtuous.' That was also the year I got that bad sex thing. My groin itched so bad it glowed in the dark. So maybe that wasn't a good year. And the henna symbol turned out to be Chinese for 'halitosis.' A Chinese guy who worked at a restaurant told me. He thought it was fucking hilarious. Big joke.

"It's fun to be around people who are younger. They don't have as many hang-ups. No kids to worry about. That's good. No second mortgages. No talk about office bullshit. Who cares about your office problems? I don't. No talk of divorce. Besides, I look young. Been micro-dosing testosterone. I think we have a really solid group this year. They have to send their photos and they have to pay in cash. I'm excited. A *great* looking bunch! Randy 'tis *randy*!"

A stewardess arrives and asks Randy if everything is okay, did he push the HELP button? Randy replies that he didn't push the HELP button but perhaps, just maybe, if it might be okay, and only if it would be, could he possibly have her cell phone number? The stewardess smiles. There's a glint of interest in her sparkling blue eyes. She walks away. Maybe later.

"I do have to be careful, though," Randy states, adjusting his neck pillow. "A few years ago some college girls made trouble for me. Or their boyfriends did. I somehow convinced them I was a photographer for *Vice*. I was putting together a photo spread. I asked them to pose nude behind a Lido's. They were really into it. The problem was my disposable single-use camera. It didn't look 'professional' enough. So that was hard to talk my way out of. They chased me and I escaped. I still have the pictures in a special album.

"Speaking of which," Randy says, unclasping his seatbelt. "Time for me to make myself young! I look much younger than thirty-four, but my teeth are yellow. I'll *admit* to that. Everyone in my family has yellow teeth. PopPop had yellow teeth until they fell out. Then he had yellow dentures. I could never understand that. That's why you buy white teeth! He was an idiot. So I bleach. And I wear a baseball cap backwards. I can easily pass for twenty-two, twenty-four at the most, especially with a ton of face lotion. I'll see you in a half hour."

Randy slaps on his Orioles baseball cap, twists it backwards, and slides into the aisle.

"I'm gonna look so goddamn sweet, gay guys will fucking want to sleep with me! I'm not gay. I've had *one* homosexual experience. I fucked a male deer. I should say that I *dreamed* I fucked a male deer. I love deer. We shook hands afterwards. I have no problem with gays. Here's the thing about me: I'm way more into the *rose* than the *hose*!"

With that, Randy heads on back to the lavatory. There's work to be accomplished.

It's Spring Break.

Before he does so, however, Randy gives a hearty wink to the stewardess who, surprisingly, doesn't seem to return his generous display of affection.

Maybe later.

For Randy and his friends at the Frog Cave, it's almost time for *one* thing:

F-U-N.

And that spells *fun*!

Ideas for New Drinks at Club Seacrets in Ocean City, Maryland

Pain in de Ass

BJ in a Motel Bed

Suck It, Lick It, Flick It

The Unpopped Cherry (non-alcoholic)

Sand in the Cracks

The Idiotic, Moronic Lifeguard

Burnt Neck (spicy)

Sun Poisoning (extra spicy)

Hard-Shell Crabs Done Gone Bad

Flat-Out Bananas!

The Horny-Moan

Caffeinated Enema

Kissing the Royal Pudding

Chapter Six: BACK TO WORK

"**M**. Night Shyamalan is a genius," proclaims Randy, walking at a very brisk and healthy pace along the C+O Canal path, just outside Seneca, Maryland.

Randy does this at least once a week, for both the fresh air and for the exercise. Randy doesn't believe in gyms. They're "scams."

It's Spring in Maryland at last. There's a bounce to Randy's already mammoth step.

Randy is wearing a pair of orange Under Armour HeatGear Training shorts and a Washington Capitals tank top. On his feet are his preferred pair of walking shoes: unlaced yellow Converse Voltages, purchased from an online Japanese seller of vintage sneakers. In order to avoid paying the Maryland state tax, Randy shrewdly has most of his special packages—including illegal Mexican fireworks—sent to his p.o. box at the Landmark Towers in Alexandria, Virginia.

The air is thick with humidity. Cicadas buzz from the loamy shores of the Potomac. The heat and *hssssssing* don't at all lessen Randy's ability to expound on any topic. He's just returned home early from Spring Break at the Frog Cave.

"Wasn't a good fit this year. Very disappointing. Typically I'll hook up with a few Bettys. Only *one* this time. A freak with a Tweety Bird tattoo just above her nest. So that sucked.

"There was a . . . situation."

He pauses.

"More like a snafu. That means 'situation normal, all fudged up.' Okay, so I invited a homeless dude into the Frog Cave. Nice guy named Benjy. Super sweet. Not one of those homeless with an attitude. Just a dude a bit down on his luck. I felt bad for him. He was sleeping in front of the Bojangle's where I always get my morning biscuits. I asked him to come back to the Cave and sleep on the couch. At first, he was real popular. The kids were asking about his life. *Amazing* stories! Great stuff. We all went out clubbing the first night. Benjy decides to stay home. When we came back to the house,

Benjy was j'ing off to a birthing documentary he was watching on the Discovery channel. The kids flipped. Then he stole every goddamn item in the house while we were fighting.

"They voted me out. *Of my own damn rented house!* Shit. You were there. You saw it! Incredible. As if it's a reality show! I locked 'em all out and took a Spirit home. Kept the money. Doesn't matter. This is better. I'm not wasting any more time on childish pursuits."

He pauses. "So, what was I telling you earlier? It was extremely important. I forget."

When he's reminded, he nods and launches right back into it. "Oh yeah! I've seen every movie M. Night Shyamalan ever made. He's *so* underrated. From what I've read, he's a modest guy. I thought *The Village* was a work of art. I was blown away by that last scene. No planes are allowed to fly over the village. Wow! Consider my mind blown to the bone!"

Randy pulls out a well worn piece of yellow, lined paper.

"This is my Underrated List," he says. "I've been keeping it for the longest time. Things that I find underrated and unfairly abused. *Inspector Gadget*. The movie. Cheese in the crust pizza. The word 'crispy' to describe something really, really fucking cool. Hermit crabs. *Young* hermits, not oldsters. Clean and odorless women. Deaf girls. Not sure why. Maybe they're vulnerable. Billy Baldwin. He's not as puffy as the rest of those jokers. The pasta at American Girl Doll in Tysons. I love the atmosphere. Best-ever chicken tenders, too. I used to go all the time until I was kicked out. Great place to write. *Who Framed Roger Rabbit*. *Spider-Man* by U2. Unbelievably underrated. The Phil Collins movie *Buster*. He started out as an actor. No one knows that. He can make really strange faces. He's hilarious. Having sex with a strobe light blasting. Looks like you're moving in slow motion. The Aussie Four Course Meal at the Gaithersburg Outback. The Bloomin' Onions are a famous Australian dish. Cinnamon Schnapps with exactly one ice cube. Has to be a *round* cube with a hole in it. The Thanksgiving buffet at Mustang's Gentlemens Club. Condoms with polka dots. You can get those at the dollar store. College students love 'em! Kid Creole and the Coconuts. Best party music, bar none! The last Huey Lewis album. *Plan B*. Genius. I love indoor hammocks. The mud wrestlers at the Annapolis Renaissance Festival. They're nuts! They throw mud at each other! Makes me

43

laugh like a hyena!"

Randy imitates how a hyena might laugh. It's extraordinarily funny.

After a good thirty seconds, Randy folds his piece of lined, yellow paper and places it back into the deep-set pocket of his shorts. He's been working on this list for years and shall continue to work on it.

He immediately pulls out another piece of lined, yellow paper. It, too, is well worn. "And here are some things I *despise*. You've heard a few already. The Salvation Army. It's a pyramid scam. Overripe oranges. They make me sick. Do gooders. I *hate* do gooders. Keep the good to yourself. It should be clear that *your* good ain't *my* good. Dancing. Hate it. I'm sporting way too huge a pair of sizzlers to dance. Michael Jackson was overrated. Too pleased with himself. A showoff. I don't like homeless without patter or skills. Can you give me something in return? If I'm going to touch your dirty claws when I hand you a dime or a quarter, can you at least make it worth my while? That's why I liked Benjy. Great stories. Until he stole everything. Skin tags. Gross. Brash and arrogant women. *Did someone drop you on your vagina when you were a baby? Why so angry?* Knowing them is like riding down Splash Mountain but without the water and more of the craziness. Balloon-animal artists. Just give me a goddamn balloon already! Riddles. Just give me the fucking answer already! I'm probably smarter than you anyway.

"The Slurpee vape flavor. Tastes absolutely nothing like a real 7-Eleven Slurpee. That creepy Canadian accent. Oh! You know what I really fucking *hate*? Lizards. They! *Suck*!"

Randy is twirling a black fidget spinner between his right thumb and forefinger. He finds this relaxing. He's been doing so for the past hour, even on the drive over, one hand on the wheel. He's also been known to do so while making love. Keeps him "laser focused."

"Let me explain lizards. Where do I even start? I'm an easy gagger. I'm talking odors. Bad smells. I hate walking into public bathrooms. I only do so now for the paper towels. I hate zoos. I hate the smell of animal fecal matter. *Hate* it. Especially if it's not my own. But I *love* animals. And I always wanted a pet. *Dilemma*. I had a pet before, but it only lasted a day. A capybara, the largest rodent in the world. I fed it a few too many jellybeans and it died young.

"What to do? I see a *Fox* report on *lizards*. Very quiet. No harsh smells. Easy to take care of. They live a long time—sometimes *too* long. A lot of bang for the buck. So I go on to Craigslist. A kid in Frederick is selling one. I talk him down from $200 to $100. He throws in a terrarium and all that other crap. I take the lizard home and name him Turk, which is the name of an elementary school friend who later became the ball boy for the Bullets. We're still great Facebook friends. Yeah, Turk the Liz is quiet. *Real* fucking quiet. Doesn't do a thing. Tedious.

"But then I'm thinking: *What could such a useless animal be good for?* You ever see all those animals who make millions? The cat who plays the piano? The parrot who does the rap? All that shit? I thought: *I want to turn Turk into that!* Make him do something for all those unwashed pebbles that I'm stealing from the Falls Road public golf course and then putting into his terrarium.

"The great thing about lizards is that they're slow. They allow you to do whatever the fuck you want. Not like dogs. Or cats. Or capybaras. I first tried 'Sad Lizard.' That didn't work. Maybe a few hundred hits. Then I tried 'Happy Lizard.' That didn't work. Turk only looked bored. Then I really studied him. *Who in the hell does he look like?* And you know who he really looked like? I'll tell you."

A young, female jogger approaches. She's attractive.

Randy, as he typically does when confronted with female beauty, offers up his right arm to high-five. It's a generous gesture. She passes.

"They'll slap half the time. This Betty chose not to. Maybe she didn't see. Maybe she's stuck up. Either way, it's cool. So I'm looking at Turk and I'm stoned from Bennies, really whoosh-zipping, and I see in my mind one of my all-time favorite historical characters: Dirk Diggler. I love that guy. I also *know* what's it like to be different. I don't have a huge cock but I do have an oversized personality and a jumbo-sized mind."

Another female jogger approaches. This one, too, is young and attractive. Randy notices but very suavely refuses to make a move.

"Not my type. Too fat. But acceptable face. B. Maybe B minus, which is pretty damn good. So I have a lizard who looks like Dirk Diggler. *Now* what? He doesn't have a huge cock. Not many lizards do. But that's an easy fix.

"I buy the web rights to TurkWiggler.com. No one's already snagged it. Incredible! Just insane. It's the *perfect* name for a lizard porn star! Got some string. Some clay. An adorable tiny red glass bead. I fashion the homemade cock and strap it on. And it looks *amazing*. Phenomenal. First time in history that a lizard has a colossal choad. Ready to fuck the shit out of anything that crosses its tiny little path. *I just did something even God wasn't able to do!*

"I take a million and a half photos. I upload them all to the site. Try to drum up some interest on Twitter and Instagram. Offered T-shirts with Turk Wiggler on it. Cost a fortune! Beer cozies. *Nothing*. Disappointing as hell!

"Then the Animal Cruel Association gets involved, or whatever they're fucking called. Another bunch of do-gooders! They were upset about the fake cock. It was erect. Limp would have fine. Erect wasn't. Too many rules! Whatever. I still have the Turk Wiggler T-shirts and bumper stickers, beer cozies, key-chains. You can have 'em all if you're interested. Half off."

He sighs. Over the years, Randy has suffered very few creative failures, but this one, in particular, stings.

"Look, I think the most important thing is that you just try and keep moving *forward*. I'm tired. Let's head back."

Randy turns around and starts the long walk back to where he's parked, a quarter mile away in a dirt parking lot. There's a rare sadness in his eyes. But it disappears when an attractive jogger approaches—the same from earlier who surprisingly refused Randy's incredibly generous offer of a high-five.

She, too, is heading back from whence she started.

Randy offers up his muscular hand once again, more forcefully than the first go-round. On his part, there is no hesitation.

On the young woman's face, surprisingly, there *is* a flicker of hesitation: *Should I or shouldn't I?*

Oh, what the hell!

A decision has been made.

One she will never regret.

The slap is strong. The noise resounds.

"Life works out if you last long enough," Randy declares, a smile back on his handsome face. "The trick is you can't stop. Never, *ever* stop. Hang on a sec. I need to stop. There's a rock in my shoe."

Randy skillfully takes care of the situation and continues talking and walking with his unlaced yellow sneakers.

"I ended up dropping Turk off at the front of the Salvation Army store on the Pike. Left a note in an empty adult diaper box. Idiots called me. Ordered me to pick Turk up. That's why I hate the Salvation Army. It's a con. A pyramid scam. Ended up just leaving him in Cabin John Park. Not sure I remembered to take off his fake cock. I think it was *still* erect! Maybe it'll help him get laid. Ha! *Ha!*"

Randy imitates how a lizard might laugh. It's not difficult to imagine Randy one day opening for his all-time favorite stand-up, Dane Cook.

That familiar bounce has returned to Randy's step. Back to the Hummer he walks—nay, *glides*. Dusk is beginning to settle and the buzz of cicadas kicks up a notch.

And yet, far away—farther than any average human could ever hope to bridge—Randy has already retreated into his head, swimming, floating, whirling admist his exceptional, careening thoughts.

Ha ha! laughs Randy. *Ha ha!*

One can only look on in enraptured wonder.

More Underrated Things

Taking a shit while wearing a fancy top hat

Getting fuzzy on mojitos

The game "fuck, fight, or tickle"

The PopPerks at Doc Popcorns

Women's underarms

Funny jokes and things

Listening to the Sports Junkies while hot-tubbing

"My fellatio kit"

Micro-dosing testosterone

Sitting on the hill across from the Pooks Hill Marriott, watching the prom dates arrive in their rented limos

Getting high and playing digital foosball

Fantasizing about having an alien pet

My diploma from drunk driving school

The satin crew jacket from my favorite movie "Life is Beautiful" that I once bought off ebay for $14

Hot-ass ethnic nurses

Tanning booth prices in August

Subletting Ocean City Airbnbs

The garlic knots at the Watering Hole

Lazy Monday mornings in bed

The Hand Jive scene from "Grease"

Going shirtless in Montgomery Mall

Frickles

Lt. Dan's Hot Beef Bites

"Girls" by the Beasties. Best lyrics ever.

Beeping your car horn as you pass a dog taking a shit

All that sideways shooting in "Boondock Saints"

Throwing a dart at a map of Maryland and then calling
someone you don't know in that town and pretending you
can't speak English

Chapter Seven: MAM-MAM

"Mam-Mam was sick for a long, long time," Randy states, standing on his front balcony, overlooking the development that sits at the foot of the hill on which his town home is handsomely perched.

Randy is wearing pajamas shorts and flip-flops.

This is *Randy's* world. He created it. At the very least, he helped birth it into being with his unselfish willingness to upload his family's long-held land and farm house for "more than seven figures, less than eight, but still enough to strut."

"I always thought that after Mam-Mam died, she'd be cremated and have her ashes blown out of a pneumatic T-shirt gun. It's just a dream I had. Maybe I'd blow them from an overpass onto the Beltway, where she traveled every day to work when she was younger. Or explode them into the Panera Bread on East Jefferson that always gave her the extra cucumbers on her smoked turkey. They were super nice to her. Not everyone was.

"But, no. The fuckheads on PopPop's side—all his cousins, nieces, nephews, all the dipshits—put the stomp on that idea. They're not creative types. My family and me, we're not exactly on the same creative wavelength. They're a bunch of normals. *Straights*. Working the nine to five . . . and *happily*! Can you imagine? Working in an office park crunching numbers? Or writing political legislation?"

Randy draws out the word "legislation" in an amusing, cartoonish way. It comes out sounding half Mickey Mouse, half Daffy Duck.

He spits between his bottom teeth in a masculine manner.

"That straight world ain't for me. I've always wanted *more* out of life. For me to be happy, my legacy needs to *last*. This is important to me. I want my legacy to outlast the great Dandy Randy himself."

He points to himself. His meaning is clear.

"PopPop's side wanted to turn the farm into a park. A *playground*. They claimed that there was this *special* spider. It was protected. That, *even if I wanted to,* I couldn't sell the farm! Because this *special* spider lived right here on the land. I took care of *that* special problem!"

Randy motions as if shooting down a row of spiders with a machine gun.

"Wah *wah*! Bang *bang*! Bye *bye*!"

Randy put down the imaginary machine gun and waves hello to a neighbor.

"That's Mrs. T._____," he declares. "I know everyone who lives in this development. I'm the president of the neighborhood association. *Der commandant*. One of my rules is that everyone has to hang a funny flag. Mine is a crab wearing a Terps hat. Mrs. T.____ has the O's bird giving the finger. I love it all.

"The association, which consists of maybe one-tenth of the entire development, meets once a month at my place. I come up with all the rules. No one else. They wouldn't have it any other way. Everyone loves it. We eat, drink, gab. It's my favorite night of the month. We're *family*. The next party is gonna be a crab boil!"

Miss Y._____, an attractive middle-aged woman out walking her chocolate Labradoodle, calls up to Randy: "Randy, we have to talk about the winter fund for the snow shoveling."

"That can wait, darlin'," says Randy. "We have months. But first we have to talk about the funny mailboxes! Gonna be mandatory!"

"*Darlin'*?" asks Miss Y.___. "Well, okay then."

"She's real nice," says Randy, as Miss Y.___ walks away. "But not as playful as I like from my kittens. I like 'em *super* rambunctious. As for Mam-Mam, everyone knew she was dying. I hired a hospice nurse to make her last days as comfortable as possible. I couldn't afford to hire a real nurse, so I found me one in front of the Highs where the day workers congregate. A very nice Mexican named Valentina. I think she's Mexican. I never asked. Actually, her name might not have been Valentina. I gave her an incentive: 'The longer Mam-Mam lives, the more money you're gonna make.' Her eyes lit up. By the end, she was making $11 an hour. That's great! Mam-Mam eventually died and I wanted to ask for my money back but you can't do that. It's the only profession with a zero percent success rate. Pathetic. Anyway, Valentina wasn't trained but she made *amazing* rice and chicken. A rose con popo, or something.

"It's funny. Mam-Mam just kept getting more and more woofy.

Sick with the goofy goof. She would call me 'Jimmy' and her cat 'Sponge.' She never owned a cat. She started screaming out the wrong answers to *Wheel of Fortune*, but truthfully she did that before. She began to water her plastic plants. She refused to eat the popcorn we used to love, sprinkled with Old Bay. I've always despised old people! Not Mam-Mam but the rest. Too many 'what's'? That smell of hard candy and talc. Their milky eyes. It's like watching someone race a marathon in a wheelchair. They're gonna reach the finish line before anyone else, they're gonna win. But so what? Is that an *accomplishment*? Meanwhile, it's annoying and tedious to watch.

"Valentina insisted on reading biblical verses to Mam-Mam, which pissed me off. So I forced her to read Dean Koontz. Out loud. The last thing Mam-Mam ever heard was the beginning to *Demon Seed,* but half in Spanish, which might have confused her. There are worse things to hear when dying. Especially if you have the 'heimers. It's my all-time favorite book."

A young woman, down below, walks toward her parked car. Randy calls over, "You coming to the crab boil on Saturday?"

"I don't think I can make it," the woman yells back, climbing into her SUV. "But thanks anyway!"

Randy smiles. And then, softly: "She's full of shit. I know damn well she can make it. She never does anything on weekends, except watch stupid reality TV and talk on the phone with her drunk mommy. I know this for a fact. I won't tell you how. But that's okay. My party on Saturday is going to be stone-crab amazing! The whole development is invited. A party for the ages. I cannot fucking wait.

"I want to show you something. I memorized the entire script to *Home Alone 2*. It's one of my all-time favorite movies. I want you to sit back and enjoy this. No one else in Maryland can do it. As far as I know. If I stop, I have to start over, so you gotta just let me roll with it.

"Okay, here we go now."

Randy professionally clears his throat. And begins:

"Where are my golf balls? Anyone seen my sun block? What's the point of going to Florida if you use sun block? I don't care, I'm getting toasted. Great. Now you can be a skag with a darker shade of skin. He's jealous because he can't tan. His freckles just connect. Hey, hey, easy on the fluids! The rubber sheets are packed. She wants Ding!

52

Behind 'Ding' is 200 points! All right! That gives you 4,700 points. 200 points! All right! Honey, are you packed yet? Yes. Yes. . . . "

Randy stops. He's forgotten what comes next.

"Damnit! *Shit*! I have to start over. Fuck it!"

He takes a deep breath, much like any actor or voice-over artist might. He once again begins. This time even faster, voice resonating across the development, strong and proud:

"Where are my golf balls? Anyone seen my sun block? What's the point of going to Florida if you use sun block? I don't care, I'm getting toasted. Great. Now you can be a skag with a darker shade of skin. He's jealous because he can't tan. His freckles just connect. Hey, hey, easy on the fluids! The rubber sheets are packed. She wants Ding! Behind 'Ding' is 200 points! All right! That gives you 4,700 points. 200 points! All right! Honey, are you packed yet? Yes. Yes. Everything I put out? Yes. Yes. Oh, did you see what Grandma sent you? Let me guess. Donald Duck slippers? Close. Inflatable clown to play with in the pool. How exciting. How . . . how . . . "

Randy stops. He's forgotten the words.

"*Goddamnit*! I can usually do this! You're pressuring me! Stop looking! I have to start over. *Shit*!"

He takes a deep breath, deeper than the last. And once again begins. . . .

Chapter Eight: It's All a Party

The party is in full swing.

Randy is his typical delight, flitting from neighbor to neighbor. A kind word here. A compliment there. The great man is in his element, smack dab within the cozy, fenced-in backyard of his luxurious town home. Food is plentiful, the vino is a-flowing, the numerous cans of Natty Boh sunk deep into a large metal bucket filled with *round* cubes with *center holes*, a folding metal-framed table spread liberally with steamed hard-shell crabs (with their natural "mustard" included), a few key-lime pies from Balducci's, as well as an assortment of other yummy desserts, including one box of Ho-Hos, Randy's absolute favorite.

No one is complaining.

"The turnout isn't as great as I was hoping," admits Randy. "But for those who did come, they're having the time of their lives. I want to introduce you. This is Harriet B._____. She faints and has dizzy spells. An inner-ear disorder. I once borrowed her support dog Benedict for the day. Man, that went *bad*!"

"Benedict isn't comfortable around colored lights or loud noise," explains Harriet, smiling.

"Or strippers sliding down poles," finishes Randy. "Kind of hoping he'd get me in for free. He didn't. Not necessarily his fault. And he took a crap in the handicapped stall. Forced me to leave early. But the girls, man, they *loved* him!"

"He came back smelling terribly of smoke," Harriet exclaims.

"That's why I bought shampoo," Randy explains, without the slightest tinge of defensiveness . . . he's just stating a fact. "As good as *new*, right?"

"Right," answers Harriet. "Dandruff shampoo for humans."

"It was cheaper," says Randy. "Where's the little fella now?"

"Not here," says Harriet. "But his rash is beginning to clear."

"Awesome," says Randy, absently. "Terrific news."

"I did want to thank you," continues Harriet.

"Really? For what?" asks Randy, surprised.

"For agreeing to the extension on my backyard fence. You didn't have to do that. I appreciate you allowing me to break the subdivision's bylaws. It was—"

Randy has already moved on.

"Okay, so this is Bam Bam! Why I callin' you Bam Bam, Arnold? Any good reason? Why I do *dat*?!"

A short, balding man—wearing pleated shorts, a long-sleeve blue shirt, and a Washington Nationals visor—stands and wipes his hands on a paper napkin. "I don't know," he says. "I never did find out."

"And you never *will* find out, son!" says Randy, grinning. "You're just Bam Bam. End of da *motherfucking* story! This guy has season tickets to the fucking *Nationals*. Can you believe that?! Hasn't invited me yet, though!"

"I . . . I split the season with three others at my firm," Arnold sputters, somewhat sheepishly. "My nephews are *huge* fans of Harper Bryce, as you know. And I always thought you were more of an O's fan than a . . ."

"Bryce is a chooch," announces Randy. "A $200 million *chooch*! But that's *fine*. I hate National League anyway. Enjoy yourself! Eat whatever you want. Try the slaw. I bought it at the *fancy* Giant."

Bam Bam finishes wiping his hands and then takes a sip of beer.

"Thanks for signing off on my new garage, Randy," he chirps. "You didn't have to do that and I appreciate you overriding the development's bylaws—"

Randy ignores him. He strolls over to an elderly woman. "Okay, so this young lady is Mary Mary. Eighty-five years *young*! Right, Mary Mary?"

"What?" the woman asks.

"He is asking if you are eighty-five years *old*!" responds a Caribbean-American nurse and attendant, sitting next to her.

"*Young*!" corrects Randy. "Eighty-five years *young*!"

"What?!" Mary Mary screams.

"Nothing, darlin'," says Randy. "Just enjoy the crabs."

"She don' eat 'em," responds the nurse. "She don't eat no shell fish. Nuttin' but cottage cheese!"

"Then why in the fuck is she here?" mutters Randy, before making his way over to a twenty-something holding a crab hammer but with no crabs in sight. He's wearing a dress shirt, buttoned all the way to the neck, as well as a Swatch watch on each wrist, one red, one blue.

"And this very awesome and special dude is Roger but I call him *the Dodger*! Ain't that right, Roger Dodger!"

"That's right!" shrieks Roger Dodger. "I love Randy!"

"Roger Dodger is the *real* deal when it comes to tasks. Ain't that right, Roger?"

"That's right!" yells Roger Dodger. "I shovel snow and I cut grass. I *love* Randy!"

"He really does, that's not a lie," agrees Randy. "Refuses to take any money. Just hugs. And hard candy, which I fucking hate anyway. Works out well! *Right, Roger Dodger*?!"

"*Randy!*" yells Roger Dodger. "I love Randy so so *so* much!"

"Okay, see you tomorrow, Dodger," says Randy.

"Gonna spray down your dehumidifier filters!" screams the Dodger. "I love Randy!"

Randy walks away. "About as sharp as a medicine ball," he mumbles. "A real man about Down's, if you know what I mean. A true rumdum dummy."

Randy makes his way over to another very grateful neighbor and guest. "And this here would be Leigh C._____. This crazy dude claims he's Taiwanese but I can't for the life of me see that. And I'm *real* good at guessing! Where's your gal pal, Leigh?"

"She . . . she's under the weather," responds Leigh. "But I'm having a wonderful, *wonderful* time. Thank you for the invite. And thank you for allowing us to build a backyard deck beyond the suggested regulations."

"You got it," pronounces Randy. "Anything, my man. By the way, did I ever tell you about the McHilson twins? One was blond, one brown-haired? Both liked to suck on my sweaty, expanding pear. That's what I call my cock! *Ha!*"

"Yes you have, yes," laughs Leigh. "Very good."

"Leigh is an important guy at the CIA," explains Randy, proudly. "A real spook. But I sometimes get the feeling that he only shows up to my parties because I allow him to break the bylaws here in the development!"

"*Private sector,*" corrects Leigh. "Nothing covert about my job, sir. Communication satellites at various telecommunications firms. And I would come to your parties anyway, Randy! You know that!"

"*Military* satellites," states Randy. "And I was just kidding. Of course you'd show! I just wish your hot wife would also show now and again! She's white. Just kidding! She's not that hot! But she *is* white! Ha ha!"

A look crosses Leigh's face but it's difficult to decipher. "Very nice party, Randy. *Thank you.*"

Leigh retreats back to the white plastic stackable chair to sit alone.

"I could swear to god he's Japanese and not Taiwanese. There *is* an easy way to tell. But I'm not telling. Good party trick. C'mere, I want to show you something."

Randy climbs the stairs leading up to his second-floor wooden deck, then opens the screen door that leads into his house. He strides into his very modern kitchen, all appliances stainless and sleek, all top of the line. Randy points to a large cereal dispenser, made entirely out of plastic tubing and duct tape. It takes up nearly the entire kitchen counter.

"That's my new 18-shooter cereal dispenser. The type you'd find at the fanciest of colleges. *Bigger*! Each hose is different. I made it myself. At this point it's just a prototype. Cheerios. Honey Nuts. *Froot Loops*. No one's made it this big before. I'm gonna copyright it. Gonna call it the Cereal Killah. *Incredible*."

Randy spreads his arms wide.

"Take notice! Do you see anything missing? Can you guess? In the kitchen? No? Yes? I'll *tell* you! I don't have an oven or a god-damn microwave. It gives ladies the wrong idea. I don't cook. *They* can do that! At *their* houses. Better yet, let's eat out. I'm a huge fan of *restaurant quality* food."

Randy walks past Mam-Mam's old rattan chair in the living room, past the empty lizard terrarium filled with unwashed golf course pebbles, as well as the tiny plastic McMansion the lizard used to live within, and then over to a large bookcase, packed with books.

"Don't go nuts. These are fake books. Just for show. I bought them from the same place where Ikea gets their fake books. So I can do *this*."

Randy easily slides the book case to the side. Behind the bookcase is a hidden door with an electronic entry pad.

It's all very James Bond.

Randy types his special six-number code into the pad (696969), a beep resounds, and the door swings open with a lovely click.

Randy enters.

"This is my panic room. Ain't it something? I'm at peace here. Not a soul to bother me." He points to the flat-screen television that hangs next to a framed poster of the 1990s hard rock group Tin Machine, one of Randy's favorites. "That poster is signed by everyone except David Bowie," Randy says proudly.

"So this is where I do my best sex watching," he continues. "Total privacy. Take a seat on the carpet. The room's empty except for the TV. I don't want it *too* comfortable. Otherwise I'd *never* leave!"

Randy picks up a very large remote and presses "ON." A video appears on the flat-screen. It's paused.

Randy presses "PLAY."

At first, the video is difficult to make out. It's grainy. It's dark. One can see pinpoints of lights flickering, all in the distance, hazy.

"Ocean City. 2015. I rented a drone from a guy named Boardwalk Billy. Flew it above the beach at night. Saw some things no one else ever has ever seen. I couldn't believe how great it was. College students fucking. It's a documentary. I turned on the infrared. Green shadows going at it. But the *clarity*. You're the first person to ever see this. It's gonna be huge. Voyeur is the *hottest* thing. And porn parodies. They're popular again! I mean, I've been beatin' that tambourine for years! Everything old is *new* again!"

Randy takes a seat on the plush rug. He is an auteur admiring his own work, knowing every delicious detail, mouthing along to the sexy dialogue that he imagines could very well be taking place on the sand between the various young lovers.

The video makes more sense now.

It quickly becomes erotic.

"My legal troubles are over. Pure pleasure from here on out.

Going to sell this one at conventions and online through my Facebook page. I can see it becoming an underground hit. I have so many movie ideas. I *will* make something soon! God, I have such a *fever* to create! This movie is just the beginning! I GOT THE *FEVER*!"

In his backyard, Randy's neighbors are partying their asses off in the sun.

Here inside Randy's cozy panic room—where he is cool and safe, comfortably hidden away from any prying eyes and potential enemies, away from any unwanted attention that such a local "character" must have to deal with on a daily basis—Randy is talking only of the future, speaking only the truth.

Pure pleasure from here on out.

It is a claim that's difficult to dispute.

Randy continues watching his cinematic masterpiece, eyes wide open, mouth agape, mouthing along in time.

Hours later, long after all of the guests have left, he will still be going at it.

It is more than clear: Randy's commitment to the arts is something to behold!

Randy's Least Favorite Movies

Being There
("that ending makes no fucking sense")

Citizen Kane
("fall asleep every time I try watching it. And it's in black and white. Fucking awful.")

Manchester by the Sea
("boring and depressing. I hate any movie that takes place in winter up north. Saw this with April. She cried of course. She was always fucking cying.")

When Harry Met Sally
("the orgasm scene in the Hebrew restaurant is way overrated. Girls don't sound like that, especially in public. And I hate Billy Crystal. Thinks he's all cute and shit. I really fucking hate him a lot.")

Chapter Nine: Horndog Day

"And . . . *action!*"

Randy is sitting in his Ikea director's chair. Written on the back, across the canvas in black marker, is "RANDY – DIRECTOR!"

It would be extraordinarily easy to confuse this chair with any to be found on the biggest of a Hollywood blockbuster movie set.

The movie being made today is *Horndog Day*.

As promised, the project is, indeed, getting made. With Randy directing. And writing. And producing.

Randy doesn't lie.

"I want to see more feeling! Really play it up," declares Randy, in full director mode. "Really go *big*. You're a dude who gets laid every goddamn day but in a *different* way. Every freakin' morning your radio-alarm wakes you to Digital Underground's 'The Humpty Dance.' It is hilarious. And sexy. When you awake I want you to give a big ol' yawn and then look down at your crotch. You're popping a bootleg boner. Uh oh! Here we go . . ."

The actor is a forty-something named Tony W._____, famous in the Maryland area for his impressive work on the dinner-theater circuit. His past roles include "Anti-Semitic Cossack" from *Fiddler on the Roof* and "Second Juggler" from *Barnum*, both at Toby's Dinner Theater in Olney. As a full-time gig, Tony works as a senior analyst at the IRRC, the Investor Responsibility Research Center, in Dupont Circle. He evaluates large institutional proxy reports. Randy found Tony on TaskRabbit.

"Rub your eyes. You're exhausted. *'Oh no, I have to fuck all day again?!'* It's a burden. A burden I can certainly *understand!*" Randy giggles.

We're in the back room of the Baskin-Robbins Ice Cream in Cabin John Mall. Typically, this small space is used only for children's birthday parties, but today it has been transformed—almost magically—into the absolute *perfect* location for a porn parody shoot.

"I was going to shoot at my own home, but the insurance costs are way too fucking prohibitive. This way, if something happens, Baskin-Robbins is responsible. I paid the manager to come down with a really bad case of 'I had no idea!' *'Hey! Did you know that they were shooting a porno in your birthday room!' 'What? No! I had NO idea! I thought it was just a birthday party for a naked guy!'* I'm paying a bundle. In cash. Whatever. The lighting is perfect. And the free ice cream is great! Bingo *bango*!"

The crew today consists of Randy using his iPhone as a camera. The set has a very professional feel.

"Tony, you have a smear of Rocky Road on both bottom cheeks, let's clean that," Randy barks to his actor, then calls for a five minute break as Tony wipes down his behind with a single Wet Nap.

After this showbiz task is completed (Tony has clearly done this before), Randy bellows through cupped hands made to resemble a temporary bullhorn: "Okay! Let's really *feel* this one."

Randy presses the play button on his portable CD player, and the deep, rich sounds of "Humpty Dance" spring forth. "Tony, you're just waking up. *'Oh no, not again! Another day of scrumping?! Ah, I can't bear it!'* And . . . *action*!"

"Ugh! I'm so tired! Not again! I have to fuck all day. I don't know how many more days I can take this!" exerts Tony, in character as Phil Cummers, horny meteorologist. "My penis is so sore from fucking all day. Maybe I will try a new location for fucking? Perhaps in the town square?"

"Good," says Randy. "That was . . . good. But let's take it again. This time even more accentuated. *Really* sell it. And . . . *action*!"

"Humpty Dance" again starts. This is Tony's cue to begin the scene. He sits up from the rented cot and rubs the sleep out of his eyes. "Ugh! I can't believe how tired I am! I have to fuck all day! No! Not again! I'm so tired of fucking! My penis hurts! It hurts from fucking all day!"

"And . . . cut! *Per-fuck-tion*!" declares Randy. "I *loved* that one! Nailed it. Ha *ha*! Now let's set up for the next scene. Where in the hell is Jenni?"

Jenni, an actress in the role of "Andie MacSwallow," is working late this afternoon at her shift at Michaels Arts and Crafts. Sadly, she isn't due to arrive for another fifteen minutes. Jenni's boss, store manager Steven, is unfairly making her re-organize the Wonder Foam display.

Randy peeks his head out and onto the main floor of the Baskin-Robbins. He calls: "Susan! Susan! You here?"

A teenager in a pink and brown uniform turns around, half way through dipping her ice cream scoop into a trough of murky water. "Um, yeah?"

"Could use some more ice cream, thank you," Randy states, no nonsense. "Make it a color that don't stain. Vanilla or something? And, hey! Do you want to be in a movie?"

"I don't . . . I don't think that's such a great idea," says Tony, still on the rented cot.

Randy nods. Maybe Tony has a point. "Okay, Susan. Another time."

And then, back to Tony: "Let's prepare for the money scene. Go wash your penis."

Tony lifts himself off the rented cot.

"Jesus, man! Put on a *bathrobe*," says Randy, laughing very hard. "There are kids out *there*! C'mon! Head's *up*!"

"Your script is so fucking great," replies Tony, also now laughing, "that I almost forgot I wasn't really visiting Cunts-a-Wanney!"

Tony slips into a cotton *Rockville Marriott Courtyard* bathrobe and makes his way to the bathroom to wash his penis. He steps gingerly around a few children pointing to what ice cream flavors they want. Midway, Tony pauses, as if someone's asking for his autograph, but continues when it's apparent that no one is.

"I have to get back to the script," Randy says, pointing to his 200-page, hand-written text. "You'll have to excuse me. The next scene takes place in the town square. There is no town square, so we're going to have to sneak onto the campus of N.I.H.", the National Institutes of Health, "and pretend that's where it's at. As a tax payer, I help pay for that stupid place anyway. God, this is going to be good. So, so goddamn *good*."

The script is, indeed, very special. But this is not Randy's only script. Not even close.

Over the years, Randy has written more than seventeen porn-spoof scripts based on popular and real movies, although (until today) none has yet to be produced.

Some of these include: *Schindler's Tryst, 12 Years a Knave, Guardians of Alex C., The Squirt Locker, The Fast and the Hairless, Meaty Balls, True Slit, Slumdog Secret Hair,* and *The Zodiac Driller.*

In addition, Randy has written a porn-spoof of *E.T.*

It's called *B.M.*

But it's *Horndog Day* that comes closest to Randy's heart. There's just something about a guy waking up every day in order to make love over and over again that tickles Randy's funny "bone."

"Mommy!" cries a little girl, barging her way into the back room. "Look! *Look!*"

"Come back, honey," declares the mother, grabbing her daughter forcefully by her overalls. There is a sense of panic in her voice. "Back this way, baby! Back to the ice cream! *This* way, honey!"

Randy isn't listening. He's now wiping down the 12-inch black dildo that's needed for the next scene.

No detail is too slight to ignore. This is a man working at the very top of his intelligence.

And it seems that nothing—not even a curious child or an 18-year-old actress late from her afternoon shift at Michaels—is going to stand in this auteur's way.

Go, Randy!

"This is me at Best Buy. I don't smile when I shop. I ain't no whistlin' pimp. This is the store in Tyson's Corner. I like this one because it has a better selection of DVDs. I like to get there at 5:00 PM, after the kids leave and before the stupid-ass government workers come home from their 'work.' I once saw a homeless guy shoplifting a waffle maker. I'm not sure why. Noah took this shot. This was the same day I had diarrhea from eating too much of the fried rice that I bought at that place in Cabin John Mall. I haven't eaten there since."

"I took this myself. It's arty. That's me. I'm always thinking in terms of creativity. It kind of looks like I'm an angel. I saw an angel once. It was sitting at the bottom of my bed, reading. I went back to sleep. I don't know why people are so afraid of ghosts. All they do is slap shit off dressers. Would love to meet a hot ghost. I'd be real gentle with her. I'd then make her scare all the people I hated. Like that manager at the Baskin-Robbins who refuses me more than five pink spoon samples. I would love to do that."

"Me walking the C+O canal. I'm wearing the slacks I always wear out to bars and nightclubs. It still has a mustard stain on it that's impossible to get out. I like to walk real fast. I'm not sure this photo captures just how fast I walk but it's super fast. That's not bragging. That's just the truth. Noah took this shot. He's not a very good photographer and he'd be the first to admit that. I once saw a dead owl lying next to the canal. Freaked the shit out of me. I wrote a poem about it."

"Just chillin'. I'm not a huge fan of history. I've never actually taken the time to read what any of these signs say. I have much better things to do. I'm wearing a wedding ring because girls feel safer when they see that. This photo shows off my muscles pretty good. I'm micro-dosing testosterone. And I do twenty-five crunches a day. My crunch song is 'American Heartbeat' by Survivor."

"One of my favorite animals is the bald eagle. Another would be the armadillo. I would love to eat eagle but I heard the meat is super fucking tough. Like Americans. Maybe I'd just add some Old Bay. I love Old Bay. This photo was shot near the Fuddruckers on 355. I love Fuddruckers but I hate to touch the mustard pumps. They should have the automatic dispensers like they have inside hospital bathrooms. That's a good idea. I might invent that."

"This was taken in front of the Baskin-Robbins that I absolutely despise. It's next to a music store I sometimes go into to bang on all the drums until I'm asked to leave. That's not my bike. This is the Baskin-Robbins where the dipshit manager won't allow me more than five pink spoon samples. I need at least ten. Sometimes I'll just sit here and scowl. If you look close, you can just see the manager in the store. Knowing this asshole, he's probably telling off a kid. This is not the store where I shot the porn parody *Horndog Day*. That turned out well."

"In front of my development. This is the entrance I like to use. There are four. If you look real closely, you can see that a golf cart is entering the development. I have no idea why but it's cool as shit."

"I'm a huge fan of the Skins. Always have been. I don't understand all that bullshit about how it's not fair to Indians. But I can definitely understand if Indians are pissed that the Skins haven't won in years. I hate the Redskins owner. He has the balls to charge $15 for a beer but he can't fucking put together a winning team. He's only good at marketing. I emailed him once but he never got back to me. I had some suggestions. I don't mind a no. Would just love to have him write back like a man. I once met Joe Theisman at the bar he owns in Old Town. Nice guy. I took a photo with him but I lost it after we sold Mam-Mam's farm. I asked to see Joe's leg scar and he said no. That's cool. Probably brings back unpleasant memories from the compound fracture seen by millions across the universe."

"One of the greatest joys in my life is seeing how incredibly close my
24-year-old escort, April, has become with my hundreds of hermit crabs."

"I only drink IPA beers. Any other type is for amateurs. I love Instagram pages on beer. I love baseball. I used to play it all the time and I was good. I hate softball because only fat idiots and lesbians play it. I also hate soccer and tennis. Especially volleyball. One hit, two hit, three hits, then the point is over. Pathetic. Beach volleyball is cool enough, at least to watch. I love digital foosball. Nowadays I just like to watch football all day on Sunday. I start at 11:00 and then go until 11:00. I consider that a full NFL lap."

"This is my good Facebook friend Mike Metz. He's paying me $50 each time I put his photo into the book. He likes to take photos in front of the old Lorton prison. We first met when he sold me a videocamera from out of his trunk in a Walmart parking lot. I really fucking love this shot. He better fucking pay me!"

"This is my good Facebook friend Mike Metz again. I told him to pose in front of an Outback. He did. He goes here every Tuesday night. The people who work here know him. He once saw a midget eating a big rack of ribs which he found hilarious. Mike works in auto repair in Arlington."

"This made me laugh like crazy. Mike Metz posted this on his Facebook page. He now owes me $150."

"You're not supposed to take selfies when you drive but I don't care. I think it really captures who I am. I was driving down Gainsborough Road in Potomac. I don't remember why but I wrote it down. I did let one rip and it later made my Fart Journal. I gave it a 4, which is pretty damn good. I'm real fucking particular."

"Here's one of me in front of my favorite Fudd's. They have the best and most comfortable bathrooms. The cleanest. Fudds it out!"

"Fucker now owes me $200. This is where Mike Metz lives in the Worland development in Potomac. His crazy ex girlfriend Kia took this. They broke up because Mike wasn't into weird shit."

"Me in front of the Teeters close to home. It looks like a fish is sitting on my shoulder but that's just a trick of the camera. I like Teeters because it has my favorite cheap toothpaste and I know everyone who works there. They have a fantastic greeting card collection. But a lot have to do with death. What's with all the sob stuff? I bought a funny one for Mam-Mam when she had the 'heimers but she didn't get it. It said something like 'I Hope You Get Better Soon' and it had a drawing of a guy with one of those dog collars that dogs wear after surgery. I still have it."

"Me inside the Teeters. They have amazing free cheese samples. Sometimes I'll eat an entire meal just standing. I'm sweating like a raccoon here. Hot ass day. One of the workers Betsy got botulism from gas station nacho cheese. She now poops through a stoma, which is a hole in the abdomen. That really sucks. But she washes her hands good before work. Or so she says! I never checked! Uh oh!"

"Alley behind the town homes. You can't see my home, on purpose. That's all I need. Some nut-butter showing up to bother me. Sometimes I throw a tennis ball against the garage door until a neighbor tells me to please stop. The key word is *please*."

"Best fucking burger in all of Maryland. Habit Burger Grill, Gaithersburg. Next to pet store where I buy my hermit crab food."

"Make that $250, cockcheese!"

"Till the day I die, girls will remain a fucking mystery."

"Not far from the American Girl Doll Store where I get my best writing done."

"Yeah, Mr. Cool. That's a solid, cool $300. Next drink on me. I'm being sarcastic, asshole."

"I once slept with a girl in this building. I forget her name."

"I love comedy."

"Me looking west toward Seven Locks Road. Just thinkin' about stuff and shit."

"I like to go for a lot of walks in the development. This is one route that I take. I call it the 'Scenic Route.' There's also the 'Fast Route,' 'The Commercial Route,' 'The Long Route,' 'The Short Route,' as well as the 'Night Route,' the 'Day Route,' and the 'Round-a-Bout-and-Headed-Back-2-Nowhere Route.'"

"After a walk I like to sit and contemplate. Wave hi to people I know. Smoke a fat ass strawberry White Owl. I call it 'sucking on Satan's wee.' Think about how much I'd hate to ever be locked up in prison. Everyone's hole's a goal in jail. If you look close enough, you might just be able to make out a funny flag on the house behind me. It's a Redskin giving the finger. It's incredibly incredibly fucking funny. Maybe you can't see it. I don't know."

"Sorry, but this is bad ass."

"Yeah. Right."

"I thought this would be an appropriate photo to put in last because it says STOP. Man, I wish you could see this in color. It's amazing. Thanks again for reading. Whenever you drive around Maryland or something, think of me. That'd be cool!"

Chapter Ten: A Live Reading

Randy rolls his eyes. He's bored. Randy is far from impressed with what he's been forced to listen to over these past two hours at this writing workshop at the Bethesda Writer's Center.

The first to speak was a woman who wrote a poem about the return of her cancer. *Yawn.* Then there was a gentleman who wrote about his sexuality and his "coming out" at the age of fifty-three to his Mormon family. *Who cares?* Then there was the college-aged woman with a nose ring who penned a short story about the sexy vampire who was "addicted to snuggles." *Good one.* And then there was the weepy grandmother and her story about a blind granddaughter with Obsessive Compulsive Disorder. *Hoo boy!*

Randy is having none of it. He is itching to get up before the rest of the group to read from his own work. This is Randy's first time at the Center but he's hoping for the equivalent of literary lightning to strike: *Perhaps his teacher could be so kind as to provide him with the name of a literary agent in New York City?*

That is . . . *if this teacher is impressed enough with Randy's writings?*

To Randy, this is a done deal. *How could she not be?*

But first he has to wait for yet one more poet, a middle-aged woman, to finish her poem. It's about a television show called *Unlikely Animal Friends* and how it's the *perfect* metaphor for *all* different human races to come together and unite as *one.*

At last—after the poet rhymes "terrapin" with "African-American"—she steps down and takes a seat. A smattering of applause. It's now Randy's turn. He strides to the podium as if he's been doing this for years.

In his head, he has been.

"Ahem," Randy declares, taking a sip of water. He's waiting for the audience of six to settle in for the ride of a lifetime.

"Ahem," Randy repeats. And then officially: "My name is Randy S._____. I am a poet. I am an author, a songwriter, a screenwriter, a performer. An artist of this great ride we call life. And I have experienced a great, *great* deal!"

At this, Randy straightens his red T-shirt that features a Washington Redskin scalping a Dallas Cowboy. "This is a poem I wrote called 'Life.'"

And off he flies:

> *"My penis ain't thick*
> *but it certainly does the trick . . .*
> *Is that really why you don't like me?*
> *Or was it because I spied on you from a tree?*
> *Looked right into your room to see you undress?*
> *God, that whole thing was a mess.*
> *Got the idea from* Back to the Future.
> *Bet you now wish you could have been way, way cooler.*
> *I apologized ten million times!*
> *And even once in rhyme!*
> *But that's okay. Your boy is now nearly famous,*
> *While you're in Hagerstown, married to an absolute mess.*
> *Guy has no job, no life, just a big fat zero!*
> *Bet he couldn't hold a torch to this one-of-a-kind hero.*
> *Dude went overseas for the Marines.*
> *Sing me a sad song.*
> *Randy's got legs. Does HE?*

With this, Randy waits for the applause. While still waiting, he says by way of explanation, "The person I'm writing about was my court-ordered psychiatrist. We had a thing for a few months. I was twenty. She left me for a Marine. *Great move*. I'm being sarcastic. Ha *ha*!"

Randy makes a funny face.

At this, the audience joins together in applause and laughter. "No, I'm serious," corrects Randy, interrupting. "This really happened."

The laughter dies down.

There are murmurings.

Is this yet another instance—out of many—in which Randy is being unfairly misjudged and misunderstood by his "fellow citizens"?

No matter. Life is too short to be stung by the occasional,

ignorant rejection. And Randy isn't stopping now. He claps his hands together to regain the room's attention. What he's about to say is exceedingly important.

Full speed ahead!

Randy spreads his powerful arms wide, as if to prove that he's offering a priceless gift. "I have something very exciting for you to witness! I do. I would like to now show you my latest movie. If you'll honor me, I'd like to think of this as my world premiere. You can think of it that way, too."

The leader of the workshop, a professional writer by the name of Brenda Z._____, looks concerned. "How long is this movie, Randy? And what does any of this have to do with writing?"

"Thirty-five minutes and I wrote it. So *that's* what it has to do with writing."

Randy pulls out his 13-inch MacBook Air from his *Big Pecker's Bar & Grill Ocean City* tote bag. He places the laptop on the table and makes a motion for someone, *anyone*, to turn off the lights. The homosexual Mormon stands to do so.

Randy clicks the start button for the movie to begin, and Tony W._____, playing the role of Phil Cummers, appears on the screen. He's nude, standing before a map of Maryland, holding a cordless microphone and talking to the camera as if he's a weatherman. "Today's forecast calls for horniness. There is a 25% chance of a powerful B-job . . . and a 100% chance of an explosive sperm front!"

"Enjoy," says Randy, walking towards the door. "I'll be next door getting an everything bagel."

Once in the elevator, Randy states: "Gonna blow their minds. I'm like the gatekeeper. They need an excuse to break out of their confined creative lives. This is the key. I'm the dungeon master. You ever play D&D? I used to play by myself. That's a good metaphor for life. Be willing to take risks . . . whether it's attacking a highly-charismatic wizard or showing your porn parody to a class of Mediocre Marys and Lame-Ass Larrys."

After exiting the Writer's Center, and after borrowing six quarters to plunk into the parking meter next to his Hummer, Randy strides a few doors down and into Bagel City.

Stepping confidently up to the counter, Randy asks, "Where's Samantha?"

"She's not in today," responds a worker wearing a Bagel City baseball cap.

"*Goddamnit!*" exclaims Randy. "She's the only one who knows how to make my bagel the way I *like* it. She *knows* me. She knows the way I *like* it. Damn it!"

"I can definitely try," suggests the young woman. "How would you *like* it?"

"Everything bagel, toasted *well*, with just a hint of regular cream cheese," replies Randy. "I hate it when it's all glopped on. No low-fat. *Regular.* I fucking *despise* low-fat."

"I think I can do that," says the woman. "Will that be all?"

"You say 'that's all' like you've already accomplished it. Yes, *that's all.*"

Randy, with a crisp, borrowed $5 bill, pays and makes his way over to his favorite table, one facing the street. "I never face a wall when I eat," Randy explains. "Or look into a mirror when I shit. Why do people do that? Am I a goddamn monkey?"

He sighs dramatically.

"I don't know. I guess I should be in a better mood. Yeah. I don't know. Everything with the movie is finished and people can finally just enjoy it. It's all smooth sailing. Don't know why I'm so mad today."

Randy is referring to the fact that *Horndog Day* is "in the can," as Hollywood professionals might say. Randy has paid nearly all of his fines for illegally shooting on the grounds of the National Institutes of Health. The obligatory negative articles in the *Potomac Almanac* have come and gone. The mean-spirited letters from the Baskin-Robbins executives have been tossed. It's again time to think only about the unlimited future.

"You asked me earlier about my career arc. You interrupted me. I want to get more into that. I'm a scrapper. A hustler. I earned my B.S. on the streets. I don't have college experience beyond that one semester of communications at Montgomery College. I've worked from the time I was thirteen, delivering the *Potomac Almanac*. Ironic that they're now the publication after me the most. Then again, they're still mad at me for hoarding a year's worth of copies without delivering a single issue. But I'm glad I did that. I've never stopped working.

100

"When I was older, fifteen or so, I'd help Mam-Mam at the Hallmark store during summers. She'd pay me with cinnamon rolls. When she opened her lice salon, I was in charge of the paper towels and the comb cleaning. I still have three lice combs with my name on them. My first *real* job was at sixteen. I worked the register at Pep Boys. From there, I kept working my way up.

"Bus boy at C.J.s Pizza. Mulch guy at Hechinger's. Sales rep at Pen Boutique. Big Screen Store. Bank temp. Movie director. Small business owner. Have I told you about that? The Float & Smoke, the country's first waterbed store to sell vapes. Didn't work out for me. It was all too new. Ahead of its time. That was open for a month. Until that idiot lit himself on fire. He's now in a cool wheelchair. With a new face. *That I paid for!* What I'm saying is that I've *more* than earned my right to ask for a bagel any damn way I please!

"Oh, here we go. Let's see if these idiots got it right."

A restaurant employee, different from the worker who had earlier taken Randy's order, walks over with a plastic tray and places it on the table. Randy says nothing, merely mouthing: *Wait. Right. Here.* He accentuates each of the three silent words by thrusting a forefinger skyward.

With the greatest of care, Randy checks over his bagel, meticulously pulling it apart. He then expertly holds up one half toward the light in order to inspect it even more carefully.

The man is a perfectionist . . . which is perhaps why he so despises *imperfection*.

"'Tis fine," Randy finally announces with a Shakespearean flourish. "I should say, *'Tis adequate.* Could have been better toasted with a *lot* less cream cheese. But I'm not going to be a *dick.* I'll just come back when Samantha's working. *Thank* you." He motions for the employee to exit.

She smiles and leaves.

"Don't get me wrong. Not everything I've been involved with over the years has been a huge success," Randy continues, between bites of his acceptably toasted bagel. "There was that pop-up trampoline store behind Wintergreen Mall. That would have been a huge success if not for those two morons who broke their necks. Did you know that *clitoris* is ancient Greek for 'devil's raspberry'? That's true. I never forget anything. It's a burden. Sometimes I feel like my

101

mind is exploding. Just too many goddamn thoughts. What I'm saying is that I've *earned* my place in society. But I can be picky. I can be *particular*."

The woman to whom Randy gave his original order now approaches the table.

"Yes?" asks Randy.

"I've just come to see if the bagel is up to your exacting standards?" she asks.

"Good enough."

"Great," she says. "That makes me *extraordinarily* happy." She walks away.

"She was being sarcastic," says Randy, shaking his head sadly. "I can tell. Not everyone can. *All aboard the Choo Choo Female! Next stop . . . Crazy Town!* That dame has a nasty case of defeatism. If you hang around that type long enough, you inherit a bad case of *attitude* sickness. Just a big load of applesauce. *Not going to happen to me.* Fuck it. Let's jet."

Randy stands from the table and dramatically points to his barely-eaten bagel. The workers turn to look. His intention is clear. He is not happy. One has to wonder if these workers will one day experience great pangs of regret when they read about themselves in a best-selling memoir.

This occurs to Randy, as well. Aloud, he asks: "Do all of you really want to be portrayed as losers in my book? *Truly*?"

No one answers. But Randy has little doubt that they will all undoubtedly feel very silly for having underestimated him. Sooner rather than later.

In the meantime, a room full of critics anxiously await Randy's return. There are sure to be a lot of questions. And Randy intends to patiently answer each and every one, at least until he grows bored.

The day is young and there is still so much left to accomplish.

"C'mon. Let's head back to the Uglies," he says, walking towards the exit. "I cannot fumpin' wait to see their effin' faces!"

More of Randy's Hates

Chinese desserts like "cookies with a stupid nut in the middle"

Red-legged Purse-Web Spiders

People who pronounce "Randy" as "Wandy"

Peacocks. Too show-offy.

Married women who go by "Miss"

Those too afraid to "call a sparrow a sparrow"

Spelling

Soccer, cause it's all fucking acting

TV magicians who use special effects

People who throw up in public

Anything that stinks of old

Mr. Pibb

That "feel sorry for me face" that Mel Gibson always makes

Nudity in Holocaust documentaries

New York women

Mr. Wendel from the rap group Arrested Development

The ad campaign "Hungry For Clams"

Disrespectful Australians

Chatty Lyft drivers

Ceramic little babies

Humans who dress as food and hand out fliers

Hair on nips

Driving people to the airport if it's not an emergency

Unfunny banner planes

Stinky candles that smell like girl

Women who have to make an issue out of everything

Bizarre 'gasm sounds

That phrase "it ain't race, it's grace"

Glen Echo Park

Dentists who don't have TVs to watch while you get
your teeth removed

Chapter Eleven: HALLOWEEN TIME!

There is a nip in the air. Fall has arrived.

"Fall is my favorite time of year," Randy declares. "Gets darker earlier. That's when Randy Dandy *really* come out to play. I'm like a cool vampire. Not one of those old ones. I hate vampires who are eight hundred years old. They're annoying, like elderly people. They can't figure out computers or electronics. They can't change their clocks when it's that time of year. They have to leave the house to buy diabetic socks. Ha! I'm kidding! But that would make for a great comic-strip! Write that down."

Randy pulls out his keychain with the bottle opener attached. He presses the remote-start system for his 2013 Hummer H3.

Outside, the Hummer hums beautifully to life. It's a magical sound. The vanity plates read RNDY82, the year of Randy's birth. Randy likes to sometimes joke that his glorious birth occurred within a golden eagle's nest—three dozen feet across—set into a shallow cavity, on top of a snow-covered mountain. In reality, Randy's birth took place at a hospital in Alexandria, Virginia.

Randy walks out into the cool air and slips into his Hummer. He flicks on his Kenwood DPX302U CD receiver player.

"CDs are underrated. I love their sound. This is a mix I put together called 'Early Fall.' Spin Doctors. Chris Gaines. Billy Joel. Van Halen. Marcy Playground. Matchbox 20. The classics. All remind me of Fall. The first song is 'Rise Above' from U2's *Spider-Man: Turn Off the Dark*. Fucking *crispy*!"

This afternoon, Randy is on an important quest. It's three days until Halloween. "If I had to list all my favorite holidays, in order, I wouldn't have to think about it hard: it'd be Halloween, right at the top. That's it. The rest are depressing. I do Halloween better than anyone. I make Halloween *my bitch*.

"Every year I have a party and it's always themed. This year's theme is 'Come as You Ain't.' In other words, 'Come as a Different Religion or Race.' I've always wanted to do this. Here's the thing about me: I ain't PC. I have no time for that shit. I'll be going as a

Jew. Gal Gadot is Jewish. Wonder Woman. She's got some tig' ol bit-ties. I love her. I was raised a Presbyterian. But religion don't matter to me."

Billy Joel's "We Didn't Start the Fire" blares forth.

"God, I love this song. I think it's genius. I wrote a more updat-ed version and then tried to email Billy Joel the lyrics. I don't mind a 'no.' Would have loved to just know if he ever received it. But I heard nothing. Too much to ask? Pompous asshole."

Randy begins to sing along to the song, but with his own spe-cial, updated lyrics:

> *Donald Trump, Ronald Regan,*
> *Emma Watson, Saving Private Ryan,*
> *Ted Cruz, Steve Doocey of Fox News,*
> *North Korea, why you cryin',*
> *President Obama, communist,*
> *born in Africa, why you lyin'?*
> *"Heat of the Moment," "Love in an Elevator," "The Boys of Summer,"*
> *"Old Time Rock and Roll," "Fat Bottomed Girls," "We Can't Dance,"*
> *What else do I have to say? Gotta give these songs a chance!*
> *Clive Cussler, Dean Koontz, Maxim mag,*
> *Lt. Dan's Hot Beef Bites, Bryce Harper's a fag,*
> *Redskins, Capitals, Wizards, O's, Ravens, and Nats,*
> *Take a gander at these zaggy-ass nutz . . .*

"That's enough for now," Randy declares, turning down the volume. "That's as far as I've gotten. It's really terrific. But I do have to tweak out the wrinks."

Randy beeps the Hummer's horn at a driver who has just cut him off. He sighs and mumbles, "Typical. They're fast drivers."

"I'd like to get into the book my thoughts on race," Randy continues, nonchalantly weaving from lane to lane, one hand on the wheel, the other holding his fidget spinner. "I know this can be a bit ticklish but I want it in my own damn memoir. Here's how I feel: no matter *what* we are, be it white or black or yellow or a golden Indian brown, we're *all* fucking annoying. But we're all *equally* annoying.

Does that make sense? I annoy *you*. You annoy *me*. He annoys *her*. She annoys *me*. Especially her annoying me. *Ha!*"

Randy pulls into a parking lot, quickly finds a parking space—as is his habit—and turns off the Hummer. "I've thought about this. I mean, let's face it, some groups are just more annoying than others. But we're *all* annoying for different reasons. Like, you might not like me because I'm . . . I don't know . . . *something*. But I might not like you because you always drive fast or are super good at math without studying, you know? It's all about respect."

Randy exits his Hummer and locks it with a touch of his key-chain.

"I made a Youtube video about all this and it went huge. Tons were upset but I told the truth. That's just the way it is."

Randy walks into a store and whistles in shock. "Wow. *Weird*. I've never been here before. I didn't even know it existed until I Googled the damn thing. *Bizarre*. Where's the salesman? Aren't they supposed to be good at selling?"

A Hasidic Jew exits from the back of the store and makes his way over to Randy. He exudes a warm presence.

"Welcome! How may I help you this afternoon?"

"Ha," says Randy. "You look awesome! All those layers! Don't you get hot? Especially in the summer?"

"I do just fine," responds the store's owner. "One gets used to it. Are you looking for anything in particular?"

"I am, yes," Randy says. "I have deep respect for the Jews. I'm a big-ass fan of your food, unless it's too salty. I love bagels. Paul Simon. Bruce Springsteen. That movie where the father pretends that the concentration camp is only a game. I *love* that movie! I learned a lot from it. How bad it all was. Adam Sandler at his best. His Hanukkah song is pretty goddamn funny!"

"Okay," replies the store owner.

"And since I respect you so much, and I love the food, except for the salty stuff, I wanna dress as one of you for Halloween."

"One of us?"

"Jewish. But so people can actually tell. Not a hidden one."

"A hidden one?"

"That's right," says Randy, growing frustrated. He always thought Jews were supposed to be "intelligent." *Why is this guy not getting it?*

Randy continues, more slowly: "So it's clear that I'm a Jewish. That's the *point* of the party. Come as something you're *not*."

"Ah, I see," says the store's owner. "You'd like to conflate two thousand years of our history into a Halloween gag. For the amusement of yourself and a few of your friends?"

"Yes," says Randy, exasperated but relieved. "*Exactly*. And neighbors. So am I allowed to look around?"

"You're more than welcome to look around and purchase whatever catches your eye," smiles the owner, walking over to the check-out counter. "Spend as much time as you need."

Randy makes a motion as if to say, *Well, thank you very much!*, and begins to browse the yarmulke aisle. "Do you have any beanies with the Orioles mascot birdy on it?" Randy asks inquisitively.

"I'm afraid we don't," responds the owner, now on his computer. "You might want to try the Lids at Montgomery Mall."

"But I wouldn't look so Jewish then, would I?" Randy retorts, and goes back to shopping.

Randy has always taken great pride in his Halloween outfits, and this year—the third in a row in which he'll be throwing a party—will be no exception.

"Finding everything you need?" the owner asks a few minutes later, still tapping away on his computer.

Randy nods absentmindedly. "Yeah. I'm *on* it."

Later, after Randy has returned to his town home with $250 worth of Jewish accessories, he will discover that the store owner will have already uploaded numerous photos of him shopping. The store's Twitter feed will already have erupted with many comments—more than one hundred—positive and negative.

But, surprisingly, the negative remarks won't seem to bother Randy.

"*All* press is *good* press," Randy will respond. "And I look damn fine in the photos. Almost like a model. Did I ever tell you that I once worked as a famous model? I was the lead actor in the *Mattress Discounters* TV ads. They were huge hits. I was the guy on the mattress with the white boxers and black socks, scissoring my feet in time to the theme song. '*Play* on it, *sleep* on it, *make love* on it!' Anyway, this Twitter attention is *awesome*! A ton more people will come to my Halloween party!"

But that's still a few hours in the future. For now, Randy continues his search for just that perfect beanie.

Within moments, he gingerly picks up a yarmulke and holds it aloft. "Wow! It even has a heavy-metal star on it!"

Indeed, the yarmulke has a six-point star on it. The owner snaps a photo.

"Incredible! So so *so* cool! I've gotta get one! Shit, I'll get *two*. There's probably a deal. There always is. This is fantastic. I scared people last year with my S&M gimp outfit. The theme was Quentin Tarantino. This is *so* much cooler!"

The owner takes another photo, one of Randy holding the yarmulke high above his head like an angel's halo. Randy is laughing very hard.

"The cherry on top of my delicious Jewish sundae!" Randy exclaims. "Yummy dum dum! And *amen*!"

The owner gives a small smile.

No surprise.

No matter the race, religion or ethnicity, *everyone* adores Randy!

Chapter Twelve: DEEP STATE

This November late afternoon is clear and bright, a brisk wind blowing in from the southeast.

Another neighborhood meeting is set to take place, and inside Randy's town home things are heating up. Within his development, political intrigue abounds.

He's none too happy about it.

Randy peeks out his bedroom window.

"That fucking bitch! *Who?!* Who the fuck *else*?! She lives across the street. Nora! I *hate* her! And she hates me! Ever since I backed into her Mercedes with my sit-down mower. I was drunk! And I offered to pay it all back. She definitely took that photo on Halloween and sent it to the *Potomac Almanac*. I *know* it was her! What balls! And the TV news. Every time they arrive with all their cameras and trucks, the neighbors get all worked up. Okay, so I dressed as a Jew. No one does that?!"

Randy's long-time loyal escort, April, is reclining on a huge, round, king-size bed, watching *Grown-Ups 2* on Randy's 48-inch-flat-screen. She's laughing very hard. Every so often, especially when Randy needs a mental boost, she will pipe up with a line or two of much-needed support: "*Fuck* 'em, Randy. Why don't you just *fuck* 'em *all*? Shit, I *know* I *would* for the right amount!" She laughs, but her attention is diverted back to the movie. It's one of her all-time favorites.

"Would love to," responds Randy, patiently. "But I'm the president of this here development. I built this place with my own hands. Or paid for it with my own hands. Or with Mam-Mam's hands. Or money. And I have no intention of ever giving that up. I'm president for life. It's a fucking coup! They—the *other* side, the *evil* side—they just want to elect their own president. *Unacceptable*! They'll have to *kill* me first!"

Randy is pacing within his inner-most lair, his ultra-designed bedroom. On the walls hang "simulated originals"—color-copied art pieces—by well-regarded artists Bob Ross and Thomas Kinkade.

Also on the walls are sheets from his infamous paper towel collection. "I should have seen this coming. I *know* there've been whispers. Layer upon layer of betrayal. I *hate* whispers. I sensed something amiss when no one showed up for the damn Halloween party. Probably still upset I got 'em all sick from those half-off crabs at the last meeting! Fuck 'em!"

That nobody showed to the "Come as You Ain't" Halloween party isn't entirely true. Roger Dodger—dressed as a middle-class African-American businessman—arrived at Randy's front door. Randy, himself dressed as an Orthodox Jew, greeted him most graciously, with a tip of the ol' beanie. The photo later appeared on the front page of the *Potomac Almanac*, above the fold. After the photo was surreptitiously (and possibly illegally) shot by a neighbor, Roger Dodger entered the house and ate Randy's cheese puffs for a few hours. He headed back home at 9:30 PM.

Randy's thoughts are now popping. "Meeting's in ten minutes. Have to figure out a goddamn game plan here."

April laughs. "This is *so* funny!" she says, pointing to the television. She's referring to the scene in which Adam Sandler farts into his hands and then spastically spreads the joy over to his friends.

"Glad you're having fun," says Randy, "but I need a *brain* here. And you're on my goddamn time and my damn god dime."

"*Damn god dime?*" repeats April. "What does that mean?"

"It means that I'm paying you on my dime! Your god *damn* time! Jesus!"

April sits up. "Remind me again?"

"I am the president!" yells Randy. "I am the fucking president of this development! *Capiche*?"

"*Capeesh*," responds April. "Geez!" Her attention returns to the movie.

"Forget it," says Randy, leaving the bedroom. "Dream trampler! I'll handle this myself! Like I always do! Fly like a solo eagle Randy! But you know what? I *like* being mad. Keeps my adrenaline flowing and keeps me alive and *vital*!"

Randy heads downstairs . . . only to find Roger Dodger sticking his thumb into the base of a lit candle and delicately licking the hot wax off his finger.

"Dude!" Randy screams toward Roger Dodger. "Guests are

coming any minute! What are you *doing*?! Let's *go* here!"

"Okay, Randy!" says the Dodger, wiping the wax off on his jeans. "Okay dokie!"

"*Okie* dokie!" corrects Randy. "It's *okie*! How many times?!"

A familiar melody is heard. It's the doorbell, chiming "Some Like It Hot" by the successful 1980s rock group The Power Station.

Randy takes this moment to point to his smile, fresh on his face, as if to say: "Folks! It is *showtime*!"

Randy opens the door. There stands Arnold, otherwise known as "Bam Bam." Randy and Bam Bam greet each other warmly. This is Randy's way. He is an impeccable host, even when not in the best of moods—a rarity.

Randy makes it clear to Bam Bam that there are plenty of cheese puffs in the plastic bowl on the kitchen counter. Also, unused Halloween candy still in their unopened bags. Nothing so fancy as half-off crabs this go round. "All you can eat!" he generously states.

The living room slowly fills with Randy's neighborhood constituents. By 7:16, it's standing room only.

Harriet B._____ starts: "Randy, it's not that we don't appreciate all the amazing and superb work you've done as president of this association . . . but we sort of feel that we might need . . . some fresh blood."

Randy is sitting in Mam-Mam's old rattan chair, fingers clasped in front of him in a steeple, wearing mirrored sunglasses. He nods. It's difficult to read his expression.

Just the way he wants it.

Now Leigh C._____ jumps in. "Randy, you've done—I mean, *are doing*—an amazing job! But . . . there seems to be a disconnect between what we want to achieve here and how you wish to lead."

Still no expression from Randy.

"And besides," chirps Bam Bam, "you're so busy on your . . . inventions and artistic projects. Aren't you? Maybe this will give you more time to focus on those inventions? And art projects?"

Randy remains quiet. Finally, after seemingly a full minute, he shakes his head and turns to Roger Dodger. "Roger Dodger. What do you think of all this?"

Roger Dodger beams. "I love you, Randy!"

"I know you do, Roger," says Randy. "But it seems that the rest of this development . . . does not. And what might you think, Mary Mary? What are your thoughts on all this?"

"She don tink nuttin," responds her Caribbean-American nurse. "She don even wanta be here. And me neitha!"

"Old nanny goat," says Randy.

"Come on now," says Miss Y._____, a middle-aged woman, meekly. "Let's not get overly dramatic. We just wish to elect a new development association president. And we have the majority. That's it. Simple."

"Incredible," says Randy, sadly. "After all I've given you. How very much I wanted to give you all the good life here."

"Oh, come on!" says a thirty-something in a blue suit and red tie. "Let's just elect a new development president and get the hell out of here. Jesus!"

"I can't even leave the house without the goddamn TV cameras following me everywhere!" says another man. "My daughter in Silver Spring! She keeps seeing me on the news! Can you imagine? And because of what? *No more attention, Randy! We're done with it!*"

"Betrayal," says Randy, voice rising. "*Duplicity.* You refused to come to my Halloween party. You would have all enjoyed it so much. So very much."

"He's still wearing a yarmulke," someone—it can't be clear who—interjects lamely.

"My *lucky* heavy metal beanie," corrects Randy. "It brings me luck. Or is *supposed* to. Not today, though."

"C'mon, dude," says a bald-headed young man in a tight tank top. Another bald-headed muscular man stands next to him. They look to be a couple. "Don't start with this shit. You're lucky we're not kicking your ass out."

"Not possible," declares Randy, all cool. "I bequeefed this land to you. From my loins."

"Be*queath*ed," corrects a man named Stuart Z._____, a banker from Australia.

"Joke," says Randy. "*Queef.* Means 'pussy fart.' Was a *joke*! Relax, you Austrian!"

"Australian," corrects the man.

"Always with the damn corrections!" says Randy.

"You've done *nothing*," says Mrs. T____. "Absolutely noth-

113

ing! Except bring shame to this development. And especially with this most recent hubbub!"

"I brought you *nothing*?" asks Randy. "Are you *kidding*?! You mean no funny flags waving proud? Just look around! Are you blind!"

"We don't want your stupid flags!" screams a young mother, holding her baby close. "We never *wanted* the flags! We never wanted the funny mailboxes, either! It's not funny. It's not cute! We don't want any of it! Like being forced to come to your stupid-ass parties and kiss your stupid ass!"

"Right," says one of the bald-headed young men. "You wrote the damn bylaws anyway. Why do we have to grovel so that you can break them?"

"Your *type*," says Randy. "Your type is really *something*, I tell ya."

"Excuse me?" says the bald-headed young man.

"We're *all* annoying," explains Randy. "No matter *who* we are."

"Fuck does that mean?" asks the other bald-headed man.

"You'll find out when you read my book," states Randy, patiently. "And I'm afraid you might not be so happy with how you all will be portrayed."

"Huh," asks the elderly Mary Mary. "What?"

"You know what?" says Mrs. T._____. "I have to attend my daughter's concert. Enough of this crap. Let's vote."

Randy's cellphone rings.

The ringtone is Survivor's classic 1982 mega hit, "Eye of the Tiger."

It is one of Randy's all-time favorites. Another song by Survivor, "American Heartbeat," is Randy's official "stomach crunch tune."

"Probably the damn press," says Mrs. T._____.

Randy shoots her a glare. "Actually, it's my dermatologist. With the test results. But thanks for *guessing*. I'm being sarcastic. But not about the dermatologist. Or the test results. Post spring-break tradition."

"Let's end this. *Now*!" says a man from the back of the room. He looks officious. "Who here would like for Nora to become the next development president to commence immediately? Say 'aye.'"

"Aye!" screams the room.

"And who here would prefer Randy to maintain his position as

114

president of this development?"

"Yah!" yells Roger Dodger. "Hoo-*rah*!"

"Who?" asks Mary Mary to her Caribbean nurse. "*What*?"

"And that settles it," says the officious man. "Nora, *congratulations*! You are officially this development's new president!"

"Incredible," mumbles Randy. "Fucking incredible."

Turning to April, who has just wandered into the meeting, Randy interjects, "Hey! Just in time! *Thanks* for the help. I'm being sarcastic."

"I know you are," April replies, grabbing a handful of cheese puffs and making an immediate U-turn and heading straight back up to finish *Grown-Ups 2*.

Within minutes (three and a half to be exact), Randy—still in his chair—and Roger Dodger—still smiling—are the only two left in the room. All of Randy's former constituents have cleared out in a most orderly fashion.

"Boy oh boy! They all left *real* fast!" states the Dodger. "*Wow*!"

"The devils always do," explains Randy.

Roger Dodger looks frightened. "They . . . they were devils?"

"Relax, idiot," says Randy patiently. "Just assholes."

Roger Dodger shrugs. "I love you, Randy. I love you so so *so* much."

"We've been so betrayed," says Randy. "So very betrayed."

April's voice can be heard calling from the deluxe bedroom upstairs: "*Thirsty*! Diet Mountain Dew! In a *clear* glass! And a straw! Just the way I *like* it! Get it! Now!"

"So very betrayed."

The two friends go on munching cheese puffs, lost equally in their own thoughts.

They have so very much to think about.

Chapter Thirteen: AN EPIPHANY

"Randy! It's Randy! You are *live* on Sports Junkies!" says the voice from the stereo.

It's 9:30 A.M. and Randy is already up and about. He's still a bit tipsy from last night's mint Schnapps orgy, now well into its fifteenth straight hour.

"Long time no hear!" announces John William "Lurch" Bishop, one of the show's four hilarious, long-time hosts. "Where you been at, son?"

"Yeah! Hell you been hiding?" asks John Martin "Cakes" Auville. "You calling from the Rockville Detention Center?"

The four hosts laugh. Randy can't help but laugh, too.

"Randy had one call to make from prison and he calls *us*," says Eric Carlton "E.B." Bickel. "*I* wouldn't even call us!"

More laughter. Again, it's difficult for Randy not to join in.

"What were you arrested for *that* time?" asks Lurch. "Taking a dump behind another old age home?"

"Or in a booth inside a Bob's Big Boy?" chimes in Cakes. "Now there's a *daily special!*"

"Or were you *doo-wah-diddying* in the handicapped stall at a Dave and Busters?!" asks E.B. "Dandy Randy *always* on a tear!"

"A *brown* tear!" finishes Cakes.

As with all of his live radio appearances, Randy is taping this broadcast on a cassette for posterity. He keeps all of his cassettes within a special fire-proof safe. He came upon this idea while watching a documentary on Scientology, a religion he greatly admires for their devotion to preserving the holy words of its late leader. And while Randy's fire-proof safe is not necessarily "nuclear bomb attack proof," he does feel confident enough in the fact that it is good to last "three, four generations."

"Nah," says Randy, all casual. "Just wanted to call. Feeling a little low."

"How about falling asleep on top of your Hummer at a stop light? That happen again recently?" asks Lurch.

"In front of a damn elementary school!" adds Cakes. "Imagine how that looked to the parents!"

The boys explode in laughter.

Over the next twenty-one minutes, until the Junkies shoot over to a commercial for Tyson's Rainforest Cafe, Randy digs deep and holds absolutely nothing back, including his near arrest for making love to April within a "lactation station" at BWI airport.

Randy talks of the presidential coup within his development. He talks of how he and April are not always on the same intellectual wavelength. He talks about how he recently learned that his copyright application for the 18-shooter cereal dispenser—The Cereal Killah—had been denied; seems that an inventor in Ohio got to it first. He talks of how much he misses Mam-Mam, more so than ever around the holidays.

"Wait? Is this the same Mam-Mam who paid for your break-dancing lessons when you were twenty-one?" asks Cakes. The rest of the gang laugh. Each is right there with Randy, boosting his spirits, just good friends, shooting the breeze, showing that they're all in this crazy thing called life together.

Now the rest of the group provides their own Mam-Mam memories:

"Is this the same Mam-Mam who paid for your Navy SEAL training camp in the backyard when you were thirty?"

"The same Mam-Mam whose diabetic socks you were forced to buy in bulk at the dollar store?"

"The same Mam-Mam who'd pick up the phone and scream at the Junkies when you were live on the air?"

"WHO IS THIS?! WHAT ARE YOU SAYING ABOUT MY RANDY?!" imitates Cakes. "BE KIND! BE NICE!"

"Ha ha," laughs Randy, enjoying the camaraderie. "Tee hee hee."

"Hey, Randy! Did you hear?" asks Cakes. "I saw your invention that sucks up bugs! I saw it on TV. I kid you not: Bugs Bee Gone. On *Shark Tank*."

"Really?" asks Randy, taken aback. "Are you kidding?"

"I'm not kidding," says Cakes. "Sorry, dude! Looks like your idea for the In-Sick-Dude-Size, or whatever the hell it's called, wasn't the first. Seems like a habit of yours!"

"Oh," says Randy. "That's . . . wow. *Hoo* boy! Damn."

"WHO IS THIS?!" E.B. cuts in. "WHAT ARE YOU SAYING ABOUT MY RANDY?! BE NICE! BE KIND!"

An explosion of laughter.

"Hey, Randy. Been fired from any temp jobs recently?!"

"I forgot all about that!" declares Lurch. "Randy shutting down the entire computer network at the World Bank?! THE WORLD BANK?! *Uh-oh!!!!*"

"Didn't the Feds get involved?" asks Cakes.

Randy, sensing it might be a good time to change the topic because of ongoing litigation with the World Bank, tells his on-air friends that he's dreading the official start of winter, but that there are only six more months until summer, and that's when he really comes alive . . . "floating on a raft at Club Seacrets, gripping and ripping a Whiskey Shandy, a bevvy of hot-ass Bettys waiting impatiently on the bay's sandy shore. Club Seacrets ain't nicknamed Jamaica USA for nothin'!"

Randy speaks of his recent disappointing spring break experiences in Ft. Myers, Florida, and how Millennials cannot be trusted when it comes to their loyalty and dedication to partying "their A's" off.

There is much laughter and then the inevitable grilling of Randy being arrested a few times while in Ocean City for public displays of "in-DICK-na-cy."

And yet, as with before, it's all done in good, familial fun.

And then the show's engineer plays a recorded tape of an NBA final buzzer and Randy's line suddenly clicks off.

Just like that, he is no longer on the air.

Despite the desperate attempt by the Junkies to lift Randy's spirits, and despite the relief Randy feels after having talked to some really good friends about some very personal issues, Randy still looks a bit down.

When told that it's very seldom he appears this sad, Randy nods. He can't help but agree.

"I've prayed on it," Randy says. "That's what Mam-Mam would do whenever she felt down. She was religious. *Jesus Christ Superstar* was her favorite movie. When I prayed last night, I had an epiphany. Do you know what an epiphany is? It's when something becomes clear when it wasn't clear before. And—"

Randy slurs the last "and," gives a quick gag, and falls asleep. There will be no epiphany this morning.

Website Locations That Randy Is Currently Cybersquatting

("I *still* own the rights for these addresses. Still waiting on the right price to sell. If you're interested, please get in touch with me at my email address Numberonelover453@yahoo.com!!!")

americanredcriss.com

americangurldolll.com

marthastewert.com

newyorktimmmes.com

okaycupid.net

americancanthersociety.com

montgomerycountymerryland.gov

harryteens.com

thewhitehouseinwashington.net

Chapter Fourteen: FESTIVE CELEBRATION

It's Thanksgiving eve.

And the Mustang's Gentlemens Club in Hyattsville is feeling its true holiday spirit.

Celebratory yellow and green streamers hang cheerfully from the dropped ceiling. "Happy Turkey Hour" signs abound. The strippers are dolled up as early American settlers and sexy Native-American princesses. Close to the entrance, just next to the jukebox that is blasting holiday classics, is a delicious and ample Thanksgiving spread, complete with sliced-turkey sandwiches, microwavable mashed potatoes with packeted gravy, and an unlimited supply of all the BBQ Dipsy Doodles one could possibly consume. For dessert, a large plastic bowl filled with Pepperidge Farm Pumpkin Cheesecake Soft Dessert Cookies.

Heaven.

Randy sits in front of the main stage, a six-by-six-foot raised platform, watching his favorite stripper, Becki, gyrate to the sounds of "Jive Turkey" by the Ohio Players, a band Randy does not enjoy because they are "too brassy."

"April and I decided to call it quits," says Randy over the thumping loud speakers. "We're still really good Facebook friends but we're no longer a client and escort couple." Magnanimously, Randy concludes with: "I wish her the very best. One of the greatest joys of my life was watching how close April became with my hundreds of hermit crabs."

Randy takes an ample bite out of his yummy turkey sandwich. It's been a few days since his on-the-air call with the Junkies. Following that infectious fun, Randy is now thrilled to be celebrating this very special Thanksgiving in such a cheerful, jovial environment.

And yet . . . there is a certain *something* that's still missing.

"I think I was maybe telling you earlier about my epiphany," exclaims Randy, "but I never got around to finishing because you interrupted me. It occurred to me that I do need to pop out of a *thing*. I'm not sure what you would call it. A depression? A dip? Maybe. Only then can I move *forward*. It's like a time machine."

Randy sips his mug of Natty Boh. "What I really need right now is to bring this whole thing full circle. Only *good* things can come from this.

"I'm in a negative spiral. The universe clearly ain't going my way."

Over the speakers blasts this announcement: "Happy *Turkey Hour*! Half off lap rides! *Dark* meat! *White* meat! *Red* meat! Gonna make you *real* sleepy! Women with all the *trim*-mings! Pilgrims, you *red*-day?!"

Randy finishes his Thanksgiving sandwich, wipes his face with a yellow paper napkin, and takes one last swig of Natty. He points to a stripper standing by a small area that's been enclosed with a plastic shower curtain. The curtain is see-through and features tropical fish swimming through a garden of colorful, glorious coral.

"I'm hoping this Injun will accept my wampum. I *love* the VIP section. I don't like the riff raff in the normal area. Reminds me of Ocean City in the summer. Low-rent Larrys. Honky Henrys. I'm *better* than that. That's why I dig O.C. in the winter. How many of these other losers—"

Randy points to five men sitting in cheap vinyl seats surrounding the raised wood platform.

"—have written hundreds of songs, thousands of poems, and a play about Dennis Rodman visiting South Korea? Oh, I'm guessing, not *many*."

And then, along with comfort dog Benedict, Randy walks over to the VIP section.

"Figured I'd give Benedict another chance," Randy says, motioning to the dog at the end of the leash he's loosely holding. "Told Harriet I was bringing the dog to an old age home. That's a lie, of course. Was hoping for free turkey sandwiches. Didn't work." Randy laughs very hard. "Meanwhile, the owners here think I'm crazy! They think I have a *brain* condition! That's what I told them! And that's why I keep bringing the dog! *Wh-wh-wh-wha-whoopsy!*"

Randy acts as if he's unsteady on his feet and has a brain condition. It is very funny. One of the men sitting next the stage looks up and smiles, and then turns his attention back to the stripper shaking a plastic bow and arrow.

Randy steadies himself and continues over to the VIP section. His wallet is extended: a most generous peace offering on this most American of holidays.

"Really gotta wash out that smell when I get him home," says Randy. "Can't forget this time."

Benedict barks happily. Randy drops another piece of turkey sandwich on the ground for the dog to nibble on.

What a wonderful Thanksgiving!

As Randy will later write in a short story about this wondrous evening that he intends to send to the "ignorant as fuck" writing instructor at the Bethesda Writing Center who has never (and *will* never) "understand excellence" . . .

"My *wampum* was a most generous offering to this pretty, primitive Injun! And *how*!"

There is so very much to be grateful for!

The entire world should be most thankful for Randy S.____!

Ultimate Dinner Party Guests

Jim Belushi

Chris Barron of the Spin Doctors

Shawn Wayons

Randy's Favorite Music Groups

The Outfield

Styx

Foreigner

MC Snow

House of Pain

Sugar Ray

Asia

K.C. and the Sunshine Band

The guys who sing the Pac Man Fever song

The guy who sang the Manute Bol rap

Poi Dog Pondering

Tin Machine

Spin Doctors

Chris Gaines

Ugly Kid Joe

The Firm

Dangerous Toys

David Lee Roth solo

Matchbox 20

U2 ("just Spiderman")

Big Head Todd and the Monsters

Triumph

April Wine

Sammy Hagar

Little River Band for nostalgic reasons

Soundtrack to *Chess* (Mam-Mam's favorite)

Right Said Fred

Billy Joel ("after the Vietnam shit")

Marcy Playground

Crash Test Dummies

System of a Down

3rd Bass

Hobostank

Better Than Ezra

Red Not Chili Peppers
("cover band. Saw these guys at Hammerjacks years ago.
Place closed down which sucks.")

Toad the Wet Sprocket

Ringo Starr solo

Nightranger

Great White

Bush

Letters to Cleo

Everclear

Terence Trent D'Arby

The guy who wrote the TV *M*A*S*H* theme

The guy who wrote the "final *Jeopardy*" theme
("I only like 'final *Jeopardy*.' I hate all the other bullshit.")

Don Henley

Nirvana

Lenny Kravitz

The Fixx

Creed

INXS

R.E.O. Speedwagon
("for scrumpin'")

George Thorogood, early

Richard Marx

Billy Ocean

White Lion

UB40

Kid Creole and the Coconuts

Escape Club

Boondock Saints
("not the movie although that was awesome too.
There was also a band. Kicks ass.")

Angel

D.C. Star

Animotion
(lead singer went to my high school way way back)

4 Out of 5 Doctors
(the last four are local bands. No one knows who they are
but they're fucking awesome)

Chapter Fifteen: First Kiss

Randy has *always* had amazing ideas that are above and beyond what other people might consider "normal." Compared with others, Randy has just always thought *differently*.

"I'm not saying I think *better*. Just *different*. I'm an outside-the-box thinker. This is not me bragging. This is just the god's honest truth. It's like playing 3-D chess. Not that I know how to play chess."

Randy sits in his big fluffy recliner down in his finished basement, next to the framed and signed jersey of Art Monk, his all-time favorite Redskin. "I'm an honest guy. People don't always love honesty. But I call a spade a spade."

The recliner has five pockets for remotes, as well as a cup holder and a vibrating foot massage. It is clearly top of the line.

"This hole is large enough to hold a Big Gulp," Randy brags. "Maybe two! That's a big-ass hole!"

With his universal remote, Randy mutes his 78-inch plasma TV and the audio for *Two and a Half Men* goes silent.

Randy sighs.

"I was telling you the other night about bringing this whole thing full circle. But I didn't tell you how. Well, now I'm gonna tell you how. Sit tight. I'm about to blow your mind. You ready?"

Randy stares at the ceiling. And then goes deep:

"When I was a kid, I invented a magical land called Zyngïa."

He pauses to see if there might be a reaction from his listener. When he finds that there is not, he continues:

"Zyngïa is an enchanted kingdom a lot like Narnia but looking more like suburban Maryland. There is only one way to enter this magical world: through a secret portal that only I know about. When I was fourteen, the portal was located in the shitter in the school's bathroom. Just pretend anyway.

"I wrote a book about all this. I'm the King. *King Randy*. Everything in Zyngïa takes place exactly one day previous to our own reality. It all gets so confusing! There are a lot of creatures. The two most powerful are the Wides and the Shorts. Wides have been fighting the Shorts for eons over a slice of magical forest called Renfruck. Renfruck is weird. It snows upwards and people talk backwards, and the guards—the Renfruckers—are incredibly strong but they don't have much patience. They're hot heads. Like Italians and Greeks but without the full heads of hair.

"So I'm the king of Zyngïa and I'm trying to capture Renfruck from the Wides. I'm the best king the land has ever really seen. I open fast food restaurants and motels. I invite Aerosmith to play at an outdoor fest. They say yes, but for a million Zyngïan dollars. I can afford it! I oust the previous king, a real loser, a talking lion who slept all day and played with himself in his castle. I make the jerk move into a small condo I built on the outskirts of Zyngïa. His name is Bennett. The Zyngïan water park is named after me. Bennett works concessions. I figured I'd give the fat fuck something to do! The teens down in Zyngïa throw curly fries at Bennett. The curly fries get stuck in his dirty, twiggy mane!

"Okay. So back to this real world. It's summer in Maryland. I'm like fourteen, about to turn fifteen. As usual, I'm impressing all of the neighborhood kids who used Mam-Mam's farm as an informal playground.

"I'm a magnet for kids who love to see me doing all sorts of crazy shit, like jumping off a house and into a mound of hay, or riding my Huffy over ramps I built from wood stolen from the new houses going up all around the farm, or flinging Mam-Mam's diabetic socks at hornets' nests and running like hell.

"One day, I'm kicking at an annoying fire ant colony. I'm not wearing shoes. The kids are impressed and laughing like crazy. I'm having so much fun I forget all about the itch. It's a few weeks later and my foot is now infected. It stinks like an old ketchup bottle left out in the sun. Or a bellybutton you forget to clean for the entirety of tenth grade, which later happens to me. It just doesn't smell good. Mam-Mam takes me to the clinic in the back of the CVS off Tucker-man and the hot ethnic nurse tells me I have to rest without leaving bed. So that's when I pretty much spend the rest of the summer look-ing out the window, watching kids play on Mam-Mam's farm like you would in a movie or a TV show.

"I notice a girl. She's my age. *Is she new?* I like her look. A tomboy. I learn that her name's Melanie; she goes by Mel. She's just starting to develop her buds. Meaning she was just beginning to develop. Everyone knew it. *I have got to meet this girl!*

"Mam-Mam lets me out of the house at the end of August. I limp confidently over to where Mel's sitting on a mound of dirt. Even then, I'm great with girls. 'What's with the foot?' she asks. She's chewing gum. It smells like wild apples.

"I already have an answer locked and loaded: 'I got stabbed at a fight at the Sub Standard.' The Sub Standard was a take-out restaurant inside the food court at Montgomery Mall. The restaurant's real name was the Sub Supreme, but no one called it that. They had substandard tuna from some Chinese country but they put a ton of tuna on each sub, so I ate there all the time.

"I forget what Mel says. It was something like, 'Wow! I am so fucking *incredibly* impressed! You must be so fucking brave and strong! You are so incredible! Do you want to come swimming with me? I have my own pool!'

It was something like that. Luckily, Mel doesn't ask how the fight ends, which is good. I don't have an answer locked and loaded for that one.

"Mel leads me into the rich development next to the farm, where she lives. The house is huge and has its own pool. Her father was a government lobbyist. I strip down to my tighties and I do my best to hide the scar and the lingering odor. I jump into the pool and wait for Mel to come out. She's changing into a Minnie Mouse one piece. Soon we're splashing and having an awesome time, two fourteen-year-olds. The Soup Dragons are blasting on a boom box. I hate that band. I hate any band who wears bucket hats and who are white.

"We come together in the shallow end and kiss. It lasts for a few seconds. Mel smells like farm. Not dirty goat hay but more like the clean, rural hay you'd find on the porch of a Cracker Barrel. She's wearing pink lip gloss. Tastes like honey. I pop a bone. A tiny bone but definitely a bone. A baby bone. It's all very innocent.

"This ain't my first kiss even though I'm only fourteen. Not by a long shot. But it's hers. She loves it and wants to kiss all night! I do a great job. I leave the pool for dinner. The sun's beginning to set and I'm still popping a tiny one. It points homeward. Always follow your bone. I can see Mel's mother standing on the lawn as I leave. I wave happily. She doesn't wave back. Maybe she's seen my bone.

"School's starting soon. I knock on Mel's window every night and leave her love notes. I write them on Mam-Mam's prescription papers I find lying around the farm house. Mel thinks I'm writing 'vagina' but they really read 'angina.'

"I learn to play Ozzy songs on the slide-whistle. Don't ask me how. I just do. I sit in the tree next to Mel's bedroom and play all night, until her mom comes out to yell at me to go home. *Bitch*.

"School starts. I see Mel in the hallways and yet she never says anything. Nothing. Not even a nod. Not even the slightest hint of facial recognition. Her friends would look at me and laugh, but not her.

"I wasn't what one might call *popular*. I think I was too smart for the rest of the idiots. My intelligence wasn't traditional. It wasn't *grade* intelligence so much as *creative* intelligence. I was a creative genius. That scared people."

Randy stops. He's done for the day. He'll pick up with this amazing story at a later date.

For now, there's a fresh repeat of *Two and a Half Men* to watch.

Chapter Sixteen: ABRA CADABRA!

Randy is sitting at an indoor table within Potbelly Sandwich Works, overlooking the gorgeous man-made lake at Rio Mall in Gaithersburg, Maryland. It's one of Randy's favorite spots to reminisce. The fake lake and the snow sprinkled delicately upon it put him at ease.

It's lunchtime and Randy is talking about his childhood crush, Melanie, or Mel, his first "real" girlfriend, from seventh grade. He's nibbling on his Grilled Chicken and Cheddar, with extra cheddar. Randy has an insatiable appetite for food, as well as for knowledge. To Randy, this is the very best sandwich in the entire Washington area.

His voracious grunts attest to this fact.

"I forget where we left off. You interrupted me. Okay, so we had an unfortunate falling out," Randy says, voice slightly tinged with regret. "Mel and I broke up. Or she broke up. I can't remember. But I do remember thinking, *What is the one thing I can do now to impress Mel?* You know? *Like what could I possibly do to get her interested in me again?*"

Randy brightens.

"Can you guess? It's an easy answer. It really is. That one very special thing that would win Mel back into my good graces? Every guy does it . . . ."

Randy waits a little longer for the answer he is sure to arrive, but doesn't. Then Randy helpfully provides the answer to his very own riddle:

"You're thinking yo-yo tricks. But no. *Magic.* Right?! *All* girls love magic, of *any age.* When a guy pulls off a magic trick it's . . . it's the equivalent of being great in bed. Quick hands. A surprising outcome. Women gasp. And then *applaud.* If you're *really* good!

"The middle school Fall Talent Show was coming up in October and I'm endlessly practicing. I'm The Great Randoni. The day arrives. I'm on third. Up first was a white girl twirling a flag. And then a black kid doing somersaults. I could have watched all this for free on television. My turn arrives. 'I'm Your Boogie Man' begins to blast, my all-time fave.

"I stroll out wearing a top hat and a fancy cape Mam-Mam fashioned from out of old bed sheets. It's red and white. There's a Strawberry Shortcake on the back. I'm holding a wand, something Mam-Mam slapped together, a ruler painted black. The top hat is real. Mam-Mam bought it at a magic store in Kensington. I have it to this day. Although it's gotten super moldy.

"The place explodes. Everyone's laughing. Admit it: Not many kids would have the twizzlers to get up on stage to perform magic. I remember thinking, *Damn it to hell! I wish Mam-Mam was here and not at the VFW playing speed bingo!*

"I announce, 'Mel! Where are you?! You are the *luckiest* person in this auditorium because you are going to be my assistant!'

"All of Mel's friends laugh and point at her. She blushes and mimes, *No! No! Please no!* But it's so very clear she's only pretending to be embarrassed. Like, *Oh man, please don't pick me!* but also really *wanting* to be picked, you know? She slowly makes her way to the stage.

"I launch into the fabulous patter that all great magicians are known for: 'What would y'all think if I told you I had a rabbit in this hat?' There is a cry from the crowd. They've never seen anything this magical.

"I remove my top hat and make a great production of showing it to the audience. Top, then bottom. They see nothing but an empty hat. Just like the Great Randoni wants them to. I've got them in the palm of my magic hand. I can feel a buzz. *Electric.*

"I glance over to Miss T._____, the English teacher who hates my guts for once saying her breath stank like dog shit. Even *she* is smiling. Mel climbs up on to the stage, acting all coy. Pretending she'd rather be *anywhere* else. *Right.* I hand her the hat and whisper, 'Okay, on the count of three, this is what I want you to do: I want you to pull the rabbit from out of the hat. It's behind a hidden compartment!'

"Mel's eye is twitching all fast and flittery from the excitement. *Twitch! Twitch! Twitch!* It's obvious that nothing like this has ever happened to her before.

"I begin the countdown. 'One!'

"The audience screams *'One!'*

"I say 'Two!'

"The audience screams, *'Two!'*

"I pause.

"The anxiety is unbearable.

"As cool as can be, as cool as the coolest of Las Vegas professional magicians, I yell 'THREE!!!!'

"I shake the hat one last time for show. I nod to Mel. She starts pulling the rabbit out of the hat . . ."

Randy shudders at the memory. He takes another bite from his Chicken and Cheddar, and a long swig from his extra-large Mountain Dew. This is not an easy story for him to finish . . .

But it's apparent that he has little choice. To this day, more than two decades after the fact, what *is* clear is that this is a story Randy *must* tell.

"See, I had found this rabbit living down by the creek. It was a free creek rabbit. I fed it Bacobits and Reese's Peanut Butter cups so it had enough to eat. He was a big boy. But creek rabbits aren't as healthy as *pet store* rabbits. I *know* that *now*.

"Ask anyone who owns a creek rabbit. They're basically *used*. They break down. They age faster. It's like people who live on the streets.

"Mel begins to cry. I can't blame her. Most girls would have done the same. I'm not angry. Miss T._____ is weeping. The rabbit is hanging there, dead. Mr. H._____, the principal, runs up and grabs the rabbit to see if it's real. It is. He drops the rabbit and runs off the stage. He later took some time off to 'rest' in Arizona. The audience is fleeing. Miss T._____ is gagging. Mel jumps off the stage and runs toward the exit. Her friends are comforting her. *Boo hoo, boo hoo!*

"I'm still up on that stage, holding a bleeding, dead rabbit. I don't know why it's bleeding. What the hell am I supposed to do *now*? I'm all alone. Typical. *Thanks for the help, everyone!* I'm being sarcastic.

"Months pass. *So now what?* What do I need to do now to impress Mel? I'm in a really deep pickle here. How do I crack this estrogen puzzle? Magic is out of the picture. It's usually foolproof but not with Mel. She's a tough crack to crack.

"How do I get back in Mel's good graces? Guess! You give

up? Good. Let me tell you, okay? Girls *all* want to be *princesses*. It's so obvious! So that's easy! No problem at all! I've already created a magical kingdom. How much more work will it take for me to make Mel a princess? I will make Mel a princess in my magical world of Zyngïa! *Presto*! Rap and *tap*!

"I quickly write up a fresh chapter of *The Zyngïan Chronicles*. Chapter fifty something. The next morning, before anyone is awake, I walk to the 24-hour copying place run by the albino and print out three hundred copies. Then I walk the half mile back to school and slip one copy into each locker. I finish as the first students begin to arrive.

"I carefully watch their reactions. They know it's me because I signed each one of the stories 'By Randy S.____.' I receive a lot of looks. Some are like *I can't believe someone so quiet could possibly write something so great*! And others are like *I'm not surprised at all*! And a few are more like: *Wowy! What a weirdo*!

Typical.

"I'm in my Algebra class when I hear a knock. It's a student I don't know, Noelle L._____. She has a cleft lip but was otherwise okay. I'd give her a B, maybe a B-minus, which isn't bad. She motions to me. The teacher, Mrs. Z.____ , says, 'Randy, you are wanted in the principal's office.'

"I'm thinking, *Mel read the* chapter *and is so impressed, she went straight to Mr. H. ____'s office! I'm going to be praised! This has never happened before! This feels great!*

"But as soon as I walk into the office, I can see that he is *not* happy. Mel is nowhere to be seen. It's just Mr. H. ____ and he's screaming loud, practically spitting.

"He's yelling, '*You have gone far beyond the bounds, Randy! You have gone way too far this time! You have embarrassed Mel greatly!*'

"'Wait!' I say, all cool, just as calm as ever. I ask, 'Where's Mel? I want to talk with her.'

"He says Mel threw up in Hallway B and called her mother to be picked up early. He says that Mel *hated* my story. She's now home resting. I can't talk with her. Not now. *Not ever.*"

Randy pulls out the chapter in question. Even at the age of thirty-four, Randy does not require reading glasses. Like the rest of his body, except for his left knee, torn years ago while participating in an illegal mixed-martial-arts competition on a basketball court while riding donkeys behind the Rockville YMCA, his eyes are in perfect shape.

Randy skims over the chapter quickly. He has long ago memorized most of it anyway. The papers are wrinkled and worn and torn. It is easy to tell just how important this manuscript remains for Randy.

"I shouldn't have written all those romantic scenes involving Mel. That was really the bug in the ointment. One fuck scene took place in a horse stable. Another on top of a drawbridge. Another at a jousting tournament, in the bleachers. I also described Princess Mel's pussy as being like 'the fiery gates of Zomoloff.'

"But," continues Randy, smiling, "what Mr. H. ____, nor anyone else understood, was that this was a major *compliment*. The fiery gates of Zomoloff are *beyond* gorgeous. People go mad looking at them. Of course, how would any of the teachers know all this, never having read the *Chronicles of Zyngïa?* And it's not as if I didn't leave them copies! I slipped a copy into each teacher's mailbox that morning. The idiots were just too *lazy* to read it!

"So cut to a few years later. Mel and I are now in 11th grade. Mel's mother is looking out her kitchen window. She'd sometimes notice me peeking into Mel's bedroom, through the curtains. Or trying to glance into the house as they all ate dinner and I'd be strolling past, holding binoculars. Her mom would just shoo me away. Nothing more than an annoying bug.

"This time, Mel's mother sees me and I'm lying on the lawn wearing a straw boater and black socks. That's all I'm wearing. I'd just dropped a tab of acid that my friend's older brother, Skitch, gave me. The tab had an image of Bart Simpson on it wearing a sombrero and giving the curse finger. *How cool is that?!*"

Randy laughs in remembrance of this delightful youthful indiscretion. "I came to believe that I was truly living in Zyngïa! It was terrifying! To be fair to Mel's mother, I would have also been scared if I saw me lying nude on the lawn, spooking off blotter acid whipped up in a shed by a guy brain damaged from a sledding accident!

"I lost touch with Mel," Randy announces sadly, now gathering up his Potbelly Sandwich Works trash and pocketing a few mustard packets for his own fridge. "I moved on. She went off to college and then god knows where. And I did my incredible thing. But I never did forget about her."

For dessert, Randy is now noisily nibbling on a Potbelly Dream Bar. Randy considers this one of the finest desserts in the entirety of the Washington, D.C. area.

"Ah, that's life," says Randy, shrugging. "Let's head back home. I have to watch television."

What It Would Take
to NOT Go Out With A Girl

They listen to NPR

They're too good for "Two and a Half Men"

They have a difficult brother who's going to cause problems

Their "starfish" is too "delicate"

They love trees and flowers too much

They refuse to find Alf funny

They're better at trampolining

They're pregnant with some other dude's whelp

Chapter Seventeen: A WORKING LUNCH

"*Oooooh*! I just *adore* this skirt!" exclaims Randy. "Isn't it *delightful*?!"

And then softer, Randy whispers: "I only talk this way so they won't kick me out. I have to pretend to be really excited. If you don't have a kid, you have to really *overdo* it."

It is morning and Randy is flitting about the American Girl Doll store in Tysons Corner, Virginia. He is holding his Felicity doll and "looking" for clothing and accessories. Randy is extremely familiar with the store's layout.

"My cover story," says Randy, searching the sunglass display for a perfect pair, "is that I'm just a huge fan of dolls. Maybe I'm gay. Who cares? It's all undercover." His voice rises: "Ooooh! These are *adorable!*"

Randy chooses a pair of aqua starry glasses for 18-inch dolls, and holds them up to the light, inspecting them with great care. "You have to buy at least one item," he says, by way of explanation. "This will be mine today. When I was last here, a few months ago, I purchased a sequined pom beanie. I told Beth Anne, who usually works the register, that my Felicity's head was cold in the winter. Let me show you something."

Standing a few feet away from Randy is a little girl out shopping with her mother. Randy nods over to the both of them, and they both intently stare at his doll, Felicity.

"I'm safe," explains Randy, in a very non-threatening voice. "Show's over. I'm not a freak."

The mother mumbles an apology.

"Besides," says Randy, winking at the girl, "shouldn't you be in school?"

"I'm *thick!*" announces the girl, coughing to prove as much.

"Sure you are," says Randy, now winking at the mother. "Get better, kiddo. Okay, let's buy these glasses," he continues, "and visit the restaurant. I'm fucking famished."

Randy walks to the cashier, whose name tag reads *Beth Anne*.

"Hello, Randy," she announces. "Haven't seen you in awhile!"

"Busy with a ton of projects," explains Randy. "And waiting for the court case to settle. It's finally done. I can now breathe a huge sigh of relief."

"ACLU?" asks Beth Anne.

"Righto," says Randy. "No need for a bag. Will just slip these in my shirt pocket. Will slap them on Felicity when we eventually get outside. When I put sunglasses on her indoors she tends to get a headache!"

Beth Anne nods. She understands. "What has Felicity been up to?" she asks. She seems genuinely curious.

"She's loving the loft bed and ottoman I bought for her." Randy laughs. "She keeps telling me that she wishes I bought it for her years and years ago! She's cheeky!"

Beth Anne can only agree. "Did I not I tell you that she would love it? Didn't I say that?"

"For months," answers Randy. "*You did*. I can't deny it!"

"Is Felicity hitting the hair salon today?" ask Beth Anne.

"Not today," explains Randy. "Too much to do! And I love her hair just a little messy. It's cute."

Beth Anne hands Randy back his change. He only pays in cash, a habit he picked up after deciding, at the age of twenty-eight, to no longer pay the absurd, exorbitant late charges on his credit cards, all of which were later confiscated after Randy successfully filed for Chapter Seven.

"Enjoy," says Beth Anne, handing over the tiny pair of sunglasses. Randy nods, places them in his shirt pocket, grabs Felicity off the counter where she's been resting after her exhausting shopping excursion, and heads over to the American Girl Doll restaurant.

"Beth Anne just mentioned the ACLU case," says Randy. "I should probably get that into the book. It's also been mentioned in the local papers."

"Table for two?" asks the *maitre d*, standing in front of a large sign that reads: WELCOME TO THE AMERICAN GIRL DOLL CAFÉ!

"*Three*," says Randy, motioning to Felicity.

"Ah," says the *maitre d*, a teen with a bob haircut. She grabs three menus. "Right."

Randy is led over to a table by the window, overlooking the indoor mall. This is his favorite spot. "Thank you," he says, taking a seat and placing Felicity in a child's chair provided by the restaurant. He pulls out his MacBook Air from his *Bearded Clam Ocean City Maryland* tote bag and presses the ON button.

"So the ACLU," he continues. "As much as I hate them, they kind of saved my ass."

Randy spreads his work papers out on the table. "They allowed me to return here. The Nazis who own this dump weren't exactly thrilled that I was doing some of my best writing in this restaurant. But I *love* it here. I hate Starbucks. Too many fucking fakers jotting down garbage in their *writing journals*." Randy pronounces "writing journals" in a squeaky, high-pitched voice. It is very humorous.

"But this is where I can *truly* get work done. Place is a ghost town during school hours. Have it *all* to myself. And the best part—"

"Randy!" says a middle-aged waiter, with the name tag *Bruce*. "Long time no *pee* you!"

"Ha!" says Randy. "Bruce! My main man! How *blows* it?!"

"Blows *hard*!" answers Bruce. "Settling in for the day?"

"Working on a book," answers Randy. "A new chapter, any-way."

"Always up to *something*," says Bruce. "Who's your friend? Typically, you're a solo flier!"

"Just my biographer," answers Randy, nonchalantly. "I guess it *has* been awhile. He's writing my memoir. I've been laid real low by your stupid management. But the ACLU took care of *that* problem."

Randy pretends to wash his hands. *Swish, swash. All clean.*

"Yup. They proved that I was as entitled to be here as *anyone* else. As long as I was *truly* interested in shopping here. And that I didn't bother a soul. And that I had my doll with me. So I'll just buy one item from here on out. Who cares?"

"Not me," says Bruce. "What you having today? The usual?"

"Yes. Best-ever chicken tenders. Mustard in a small bowl. Separate. Not ketchup. I hate ketchup. The smell reminds me of my belly-button in the tenth grade. Pomodoro pasta, also naked. Butter on the side. I'll get dessert later."

"I'm on it," says Bruce. "And for your friend?"

"He'll have the triple-stacked grilled cheese," Randy says expertly. "And make sure it's *triple* stacked. Last time it was double stacked. Thank you."

"You got it, my brother!" Bruce says, making his way back to the kitchen with this incredibly detailed and nuanced order.

"The advantage of coming to a restaurant where only kids order is that they're used to picky eaters," explains Randy. "And I'm a picky eater. I'm not afraid to admit that. It makes me no less of a man. I hate spices and shit. I like things *plain*. To actually *taste* the food I'm eating. Isn't that its damned purpose? It *is*."

Randy places his MacBook Air on the table. He opens a Microsoft Word document.

"Have a *ton* of work to do," he states. "First item: deal with that stupid writing teacher—if you can even call her that—at the Bethesda Writing Shitter. Going to explain to her again, like one would a child, why I'm a great writer. And why she's *not*. And why I will *never* apologize for showing my movie. She claims that she suffered an unwarranted and distressing episode after seeing my porn parody. *Fuck her*. She wants me to give her a trigger warning? *I'll give her a trigger warning! Right on her face!*

"And you know what? She lied. She never did send my poems to her agent. She's a *fake*. So I'll publish 'em myself. Big whoop! Okay. Here we go. How does this sound?"

Randy clears his throat and begins to tap out his written response to the teacher:

"'Gee, I'm so sorry that my movie caused you to feel uncomfortable. I'm being sarcastic. Next time, before you criticize, why don't you try to actually *finish* the movie first? If you watch the whole thing, it'll make sense! I'm a professional writer with hundreds and hundreds of credits, and a very successful Twitter page. I have 25,000 followers. In comparison, the Salvation Army has 15,000 followers. I only paid for 22,000 of those followers. What have you ever published beyond a shitty book of poems on genocide that was positively reviewed in the *Washington Post*? More like the *Washington Compost*!'"

"And we are *back*! With some yummy tummy dishes!"

Bruce stands before the table, carrying a ceramic plate of

best-ever chicken tenders, cooked to perfection, with the mustard, as requested, on the side. "And . . . a *triple* stacked grilled cheese for Bill Shakespeare," says Bruce, placing the large white plate down on the table.

"Excuse me?" Randy asks.

"For your writing friend," explains Bruce, motioning with a sleeved elbow. "Your memoir writer. William Shakespeare."

"There's only *one* writer here," explains Randy, peeved. "And you're looking at him. *Me.*"

"I . . . I apologize," says Bruce. "I should have spoken more carefully. Is there anything else I can get you at this time?"

"No," answers Randy, motioning for Bruce to leave. "I have an important letter to finish. And then a chapter in an ongoing book. So, yes. *That'll be all.*"

Bruce bows deeply and retreats.

"Asshole," announces Randy, poking his fork into the mound of pasta. "He was being sarcastic. That was a sarcastic bow. Loser asshole clown with a fucking awful job who has a dream of acting. Never gonna happen because he's a fucking loser clown in a fucking loser awful job. I'll pitch a fumy dookie right on his fucking head. I will kick him to the ground and stomp on his spirit! Flick it and *stick* it! Piss it and *miss* it!"

Lunch has been served.

Felicity, from her attached chair—her large green eyes open wide, her tiny doll mouth just slightly ajar—watches the scene taking place in front of her intently, missing nothing.

It's not difficult to see why Randy pretends to be so attached to her.

This most wonderful lunch goes on for hours.
One can only hope it never, ever ends!

Places Randy Would Most Like to Die

At the head of a conga line in the Mexican section of EPCOT Center

Nude, on a trampoline

"In the middle of one of those trust-game exercises. People would go flat-out bananas."

"In my panic room with no one finding me for years"

At the Superbowl, on the Jumbo Tron

In the "VIP Box" at a Truck and Tractor Pull

In a dunk-'em-booth, taunting the fuckheads walking by

"On the high-dive at my local pool"

"Ikea cafeteria, face-first in a heaping bowl of Swedish meatballs"

In the mudpit at the Annapolis Renaissance Faire

While playing donkey basketball and going in for a layup

"My elbows on the rail of a Potomac riverboat casino, with me pondering all my crazy-ass-shit past adventures"

Sandals Resort, Bahamas, strapped into a rented parasail

In a vibrating massage chair at The Sharper Image

"Riding the Tilt-a-Whirl at a church carnival as 'Funky Cold Medina' blasts over the loudspeakers!"

At a Rock and Roll Fantasy Camp, stage diving

At a Civil War re-enactment, dressed as a private, leading the charge

At the Outback Restaurant, holding the "I Can't Believe I Just Ate 25 Racks of Ribs, Mate!" trophy

In a sweaty post-concert huddle with the members of the Spin Doctors

In line for a funnel cake

"Williamsburg, Virginia: Tri-corner hat, head in the stocks"

"Back room of a Spencer's Gifts, next to the cock candles"

Inside a Winnebago, Wal-Mart parking lot, Frederick, Maryland

On the toilet, juggling

Chapter Eighteen: A New Dawn

Randy sits patiently in an office waiting room in downtown Bethesda.

"Still pissed off about the Insuck-Ta-Side. That was a genius, once-in-a-lifetime idea. They definitely stole that idea from me. I don't know how. *Hurtful.* But my Van Halen graphic novel is coming along super. I'm still waiting for permission from David Lee Roth's people to turn him into a slow-moving zombie who loves cocaine. He'll move at a *normal* pace. It's *very* funny!

"The flavored sex lube is working out phenomenal. I've been mixing and matching in my kitchen. Kinking out some new flavors for women who dig their lube more sour than sweet. And, for the ethnics, fried and spicy.

"Sadly, my SAFE SIT app was rejected by Apple, which is lame, but I'm going to take it solo. Handing out fliers on the Metro starting next week. Viral campaign. Which is hot. It'll look like I'm being mugged. I have a black friend who could pull it off. He's a scientist now. Knew him in high school. We played D&D. I was the dungeon master." Randy laughs. "I made the guy carry all my weapons and armor. Haven't talked in awhile. But *great* Facebook friends! Hoping he'll get back to me!"

There is a pep to Randy's step. His face glows. He appears to have catapulted himself into a better "space."

"I feel transformed. I'm almost *vibrating.* Glowing. I dark-jammed *hard* last night. Didn't invite you because I needed the creative space. I feel that I'm on an upswing. And after today . . . well, I have a very solid feeling about this. A brand new day for Randy Dandy! Let. It. *Begin!*"

"Randy S._____," announces a secretary. "Mrs. K._____ will see you now."

"Kick it out!" says Randy. He follows the secretary out of the waiting room and down the plush hallways of the law office. The walls are lined with diplomas, awards and expensively framed antique photos of Bethesda, when the streets were lined with streetcars and when men on their way to work wore seersucker suits and straw fedoras.

Randy, wearing a red Maryland Terps T-shirt and a pair of his favorite casual cut-off khaki long shorts, takes in everything.

The secretary introduces us to yet another secretary. "This way please," the second secretary proclaims, leading Randy into a grand office: mahogany desk, hardwood floors, a bronze lady justice sculpture on a pedestal, holding balance scales in one hand, a sword in the other.

Framed and desk photos can be seen of a family: a wife, a husband, two sons and a dog.

An attractive woman, sitting behind the large desk in an Aeron chair, stands and extends her right hand. She appears to be the same age as Randy. Randy leans forward. They shake hands. *Is there a look of recognition in the lawyer's eyes? Perhaps she's read about Randy and his exploits? Has she somehow heard about this infamous local man and his numerous inventions and his many works of written art? Perhaps she's a fan of the Sports Junkies?*

"Please. Have a seat," the lawyer says.

Randy does so.

"Wow! Comfy," he states. "*Whoof!* Real leather?"

"Not fake," answers the lawyer. And then to the secretary, "Thank you, Liz."

"I had a hard time finding a parking space," begins Randy. "Bethesda. It ain't like it used to be!"

"No," says the lawyer. "Parking is at a premium. Did you park in our lot? We can validate."

"Down the street," says Randy, annoyed. "Jesus. Wish your office had told me that before. Now we gotta make this under an hour."

"That shouldn't be a problem," answers the lawyer, smiling. She glances at the clock on the wall. "How may I be of assistance to you today? You told Rachel, my paralegal, that you're in dire legal straits?"

"Ha! I did," says Randy. "Yeah. That's what I said."

"And? . . . You're not?"

"Sort of," says Randy. "Kinda, I guess. It's complicated."

The lawyer takes out a yellow legal pad. "Let's start at the beginning. Basic. Name?"

Randy hesitates. "Randy. Randy S._____."

If the lawyer recognizes the name, she does not show it. "Occupation?"

"Full-time artist."

"Okay. What type of artist?"

"*Life* artist."

The lawyer begins to jot down a notation . . . but stops. She looks up. "And who is your friend?"

"*This* guy? My memoirist."

"Your what?"

"You don't know what *memoirist* means?"

"Not the way you just pronounced it. Someone is writing your life story?"

"Yes." Randy shrugs. "That's typically what a memoirist does."

Randy laughs. The lawyer does not.

"Anyway," says Randy. "I never learned to type. And your boy ain't about to start now!"

"I'm a defense lawyer. You're aware of that, correct? Are you in any sort of legal trouble? And is this on or off the record?"

"Again, it's complicated," answers Randy.

"Let's cut to the chase," says the lawyer. "Why are you here?"

"You really don't remember me, do you?"

"Am I supposed to?"

"Let's cut the shit, right?"

The lawyer's eyes narrow. "Okay. Let's cut it."

"Do you remember Mam-Mam?"

"Mam-Mam?" asks the lawyer. "Um, I don't . . . "

"Of course you do," says Randy. "You used to call her *Slam Jam* as a joke. As if that was funny. But I'm over it."

"Who are you?" asks the lawyer.

"Who *am* I?" Randy says, mysteriously.

"Yes. Who *are* you?"

A grin. "I'm Randy. Randy S._____. And you're Mel. Mel K._____. Formerly Mel T._____. Ring a bell?"

"Oh my god," says Mel, her left eye twitching from excitement.

"Yup," says Randy.

"It's . . . wow. *Randy*. It's been . . . far too long."

"Indeed it has," says Randy. "I reached out years ago on your Erols.com email account. You never got back."

"I haven't had that account since college."

Randy grins. He knows better. "That's not what your mom told me when I pretended to be your doctor."

"*Excuse* me?" asks Mel. Now it's her right eye that begins to twitch. "You called my mom? And told her you were my *doctor*?"

"Years ago. How is she, by the way?"

"She's dead."

"I'm so sorry," says Randy, but makes a face as if to imply, *Not really. She treated me worse than a bug sucked into an Insuck-Ta-Side.*

"Randy, you told my assistant you needed legal help. Is that not true?" Mel's face is flushed a deep crimson, perhaps as a result of the great excitement from seeing such an old friend after so very long.

"First of all, before I begin, I do want to apologize. And I say that as a thirty-four year old man, even though I have been told many, many times that I look no older than twenty-one. Okay?"

"Okay. . . ."

"But I think back on that night often. In some ways, it was the best night of my life. In other ways, well, not so much . . . I'm sure you feel the same."

"To be honest, I don't know what night you're referring to."

"Mel. *Come* now — by the way, are you married?"

"I am, yes," says Mel, motioning to the framed photo that sits behind her. "We just celebrated our tenth."

"Someone from Churchill?"

"No, we met at law school."

"I've slept with 46 women," states Randy frankly, as if no big deal.

"That's . . . wonderful."

"Thanks. Back to the night, I was *young*. It was the magic night. The night I made you cry. The night I couldn't pull off the trick. I had zero idea that the rabbit would be dead when I was up on stage!"

"Ah," says Mel. "*That* night. I mean, if I remember, I wasn't

150

crying because of the trick. I was probably crying more because of—"

"I knew very little about creek rabbits," Randy interrupts.

"Randy . . . it's terrific to see you again. It's been far too long. I would love to chat about old times . . . at a *later* date. I'm extraordinarily busy this morning. I have a very difficult case in Rockville tomorrow, very early. And I'm afraid—"

Randy makes a "shhhhhhhhh" motion.

"You're making us both look bad. Just calm down. I never forgot you, Mel, and I'm pretty sure you never forgot me, even though you might now be pretending as much. I was your first kiss. Am I wrong?"

"I . . . yes. I suppose you were. I guess." Mel glances to the clock on the wall. She stands.

Randy asks a bit shyly: "May I be so bold as to ask: Was I a good kisser?"

"Randy . . . I cannot tell you how long ago this all seems to me. It feels like worlds and worlds ago. Honestly. Ages, really . . ."

Mel starts to make her way to the door. Randy does not follow. He stands, reaches into his *Big Pecker's Bar & Grill* tote bag, and produces a magician's hat.

"A magic hat?" the lawyer asks. "Why—oh Jesus."

"Righto," says Randy, now pulling out a wand. "In my mind, very *little* time has passed." Randy snaps his fingers as if to accentuate the quick passage of time. "Do you . . . do you ever think about me? You know, occasionally, sometimes even in moments of passion—"

Randy stands between Mel and the closed office door. Mel looks longingly at the door and makes a motion to it. Randy steps to his left, blocking her.

"No. I—"

"I always meant to ask. How did you lose your virginity? How old were you? I was sixteen. The woman was twenty-three. She was later arrested for robbing an Orange Julius at Montgomery Mall. She now has four kids. We did it in the reference aisle of Davis Library."

"Randy, I really don't want to talk about personal matters. In fact—"

"ONE!" Randy yells, magic wand waving inches from Mel's face.

"Don't tell me . . ."

"TWO!"

"Are you out of your fucking mind—"

Randy steps forward and presents the hat to Mel.

"You gotta be kidding me," Mel responds, taken aback.

Is this really happening? After all this time?

It is.

"*Pull it*!" screams Randy loudly, in his best Great Randoni voice. "PULL IT HARD!"

Mel glances to the door.

"PULL IT!" the Great Randoni screams again.

When the Great Randoni orders, there is no refusing.

Mel shakes her head no.

Instead, Randy reaches into his own magic hat, back nearly thirty years, into a past that Mel mistakenly may have felt was long over.

It isn't.

Now it's Mel's turn to scream.

"My god! It's *alive*!"

"Yes!" says Randy, pulling out a store-bought, very large rabbit. "That's the *point*!"

"*Take* it," says Mel. "You lunatic! Get the fuck out of my office! *Fucking crazy person*!"

Mel's secretary, Liz, now barges in. Her eyes, too, appear to be twitching from all of the excitement. She places a hand over her mouth. "What in the good Christ—"

And now it's her turn to scream. In response, the rabbit, perhaps a bit overwhelmed, urinates.

"I wrote this for you," says Randy, still standing between Mel and the door. "It's the latest installment of my Zyngïan chronicles. You're now a *queen*. And you may *keep* that."

He grandly hands over to Mel a thick sheet of papers.

Security arrives.

But Randy is well prepared. He makes a motion as if to say, *I am of no harm! We are old high school lovers, pleasantly reconnecting after many years. She may keep the rabbit, the one that I have successfully pulled out of a hat this time. I did it correctly. Yes, it is very much still alive!*

152

"That went well," says Randy, a few hours later. "I feel better now. A burden has been lifted. I just wish I knew about that parking validation *before*."

The *Potomac Almanac* will soon come knocking but Randy will refuse to open his front door. He has no more time for that.

This is the first day of the rest of his life.

Randy is a man re-born.

But more importantly, there is a party to plan. Perhaps the biggest of Randy's life.

Here comes Randy now!

Chapter Nineteen: Full Circle!

66 "In some ways, it was the best writing I've ever done," says Randy sadly, sitting on the edge of his bed.

There is less than one hour until the start of his annual winter holiday party and Randy still hasn't yet dressed. "It's a shame Mel sent all these papers back to me. Just *try* telling me this is no good! I'll crack you to the fucking ribs, chooch!"

Randy recites from memory:

"'*Queen Mel sits on her golden throne. The dwarf slave, MacIntosh, takes a glance up her royal silk skirt. What he sees would blind a normal man, but MacIntosh is anything but a normal man. MacIntosh says not a word in his high-pitched midget voice. He takes a bite out of his Bojangle's Biscuit. Fake butter drips down his tiny chin and then on to his tiny, adorable lap. Between MacIntosh and King Randy, there is an understanding—silent but deadly—that perhaps among the many hundreds who live within this universe called Zyngïa, there are perhaps only two—and these two alone—who have observed Queen Mel's 'fiery gates of Zomoloff.'*

"I mean, that's good, *right*? That means *vagina*. But I have a feeling Mel never even read it. She sent it back. As if I don't have another copy. And that's disappointing. Maybe she's not a reader. A lot of people aren't. She could be one of those who are only into money and politics. Not art. But I'm an adult now and I say this with all honesty: I really do hope we become fantastic Facebook friends. I just sent her a request."

Randy holds up the envelope from the law firm that arrived with today's mail. "But I do wish she hadn't sent me a legal bill for $350. *Not cool.*

"That's a lot of money," explains Randy. "For the normal person. But I guess I ain't so normal. I'm like the dwarf MacIntosh. But taller. And with fewer sexual problems. And you know what? I'm *still* going to send Mel my memoir when it's completely finished. *That's what type of guy I am!*"

He tosses the envelope with the legal bill into his Washington

Redskins themed bedroom trashcan, and lets a freaky one fly. "Remind me to jot that one down in my Fart Journal. That's a four. A *five* if I'm in a good mood. Which I probably would be after smelling that gem. But I can't smell it. I'm too used to it. Occupational hazard. Regardless, D flat. I have *perfect* pitch.

"So," continues Randy, petting his pet rabbit of a few weeks, Fugs Funny, "my holiday party is in twenty minutes. You might be thinking, *Hey! Who in this development would ever come to Randy's holiday party?!* Guess what? *Everyone's* coming. 100%. Ponder *that*. I got the *touch*! It really helps to throw it in early February. Fewer parties to compete with."

Randy strides into his walk-in closet to prepare for his special guests. His cologne collection sits handsomely on a shelf, in alphabetical order, beginning with *Alegria* and ending with *Zippo Silver*.

"Biggest collection in Southern Maryland," announces Randy. "There's an asshole in Hagerstown who has a larger one. But he's an asshole. And he's in Hagerstown."

After much deliberation, Randy chooses *Eternity* by Calvin Klein, shakes out a few drops and slaps it on both cheeks. Randy quickly chooses his outfit for the night, dresses, and heads downstairs.

In the kitchen, Roger Dodger is standing on his tippy-toes on the highest step of an eight-foot tall ladder. The Dodger is attempting to hang decorations according to Randy's very exacting party standards. The Dodger's concentration is so deep that his tongue sticks out.

"To the *right*, Roger," says Randy. "C'mon, man! This is *mucho* importanto."

Roger, ever the fan of Randy's impeccable taste, adjusts the nude cut-out Santa a smidge to the right. The Santa is receiving oral pleasure from a very attractive female reindeer. The reindeer's anus is a Christmas star.

"And . . . *perfect*-a-*mundo*!" eyes Randy, squinting. "Now careful getting off there, bruv. That's all I fucking need! Another asshole fucking suing me for breaking his goddamn neck!"

As the Dodger weaves a bit on the ladder before slowly climbing down, Randy places Fugs the Magical Bunny back into his wire cage.

The doorbell chimes the Power Station's "Some Like It Hot."

Randy strides over to the door and opens it. It's the caterer with all of the delicious food for tonight's event.

"Right this way, kid," announces Randy, leading the man through the foyer and into the kitchen. "Place all them yummies right there on the counter. *There's a boy.*"

Randy slices off a few bills from the top of his thick stack and presents it to this most appreciative of men. "There but for the grace of god go me," says Randy, pointing to the fifty-something man wearing a Lido's Pizza cap.

The deliveryman is at first puzzled but then smiles. Grateful for his $3 tip, he exits quickly. Or tries to. He has a terrible limp.

Within moments, the first guest of the evening arrives. It's Harriet B._____. Panting next to her is her comfort dog, Benedict.

"Harriet! Benedict!" exclaims Randy. "So nice to see you again! Harriet, you're looking as lovely as always. And Benedict! What a handsome fella!"

"The smell finally came out," says Harriet. "Had to wash him a few times."

"That old age home really stinks!" says Randy, by way of explanation.

"He stunk more like cigarettes and booze," Harriet says.

"Tee hee *hee!*" laughs Randy. "Old timers! They really know how to party! Take a seat, take a seat!"

Leigh C._____ is the next to arrive, along with his beautiful wife, Bets.

"Leigh! And wife! *The great white hope!* To what do I owe this rare and wonderful pleasure?" asks Randy, hugging both.

"We wouldn't miss it for the world," answers Leigh. "*So* excited!"

Bets nods but says nothing.

"*Welcome!*" says Randy, pointing to the living room. "Plenty of square pizza! Square pizza for the square spook!"

"Not a spook, Randy. *Private* communications," corrects Leigh. "Not government related in the *least.*"

"Righto," says Randy, already moving on to his next guest, Arnold, who stands before the door. "Bam Bam! *Great to see you*! *Still* waiting for those Skins tix! I know, I know! Your son wants to bring his friends! But, man, I would *love* to hit that Dallas game next season!"

"I'll see what I can do," answers Bam Bam. "Might have an extra seat, although my sick father should be visiting from West Virginia for that one. He'd love to attend perhaps his last-ever game—"

"Fantastic!" says Randy. "That would be awesome. I haven't been to a Cowboys game in *forever!*"

The rest of the neighborhood association arrives. No one appears to be missing. The turnout is beyond excellent. Randy was not exaggerating. He seldom needs to. This is the hottest ticket in the development. Before long, the room is bustling with talk and laughter and much frivolity.

The one exception might be Nora, the new, unpopular president of the development, who sits by herself, a leader alone, shunted both physically and emotionally off to the side in favor of Randy, who still officially remains the "president of fun." Nora appears to be very lonely. It is a position that Randy wouldn't wish on anyone, except for perhaps Nora.

A tremendously loud car horn can be heard. The noise of those enjoying the party—rising high and oscillating—comes to a quick and sudden halt. Randy, standing on a kitchen chair before his celebrators, aims his keychain with the bottle opener toward the front door, pressing the remote-start system for his 2013 Hummer H3.

"*New car horn!*" Randy announces. "You might recognize it. 'Fly' by one of my all-time favorite groups, Sugar Ray! Classic song! Perfect for *scrumpin'!*"

It is, indeed, one of Randy's all-time favorite songs. He presses his keychain again and the horn switches off.

"Not to worry now! This will be *real* quick! I'll let everyone return to partying their A's off!," says Randy. "But I first wanted to thank you all for stopping by. I love you all! Or most! I'm looking forward to yet another amazing year here in this beautiful development! *So many* projects planned! Don't know if I told you yet but I'm planning on hosting my second music festival come spring: 'RandyFest.' Will hold that party in the playground. As always, for those who live here, half off! The petting zoo which I've been planning with animals borrowed from the National Zoo will happen later this summer! Just waiting to hear back about the pandas. In the meantime,

157

here's to a happy and healthy Christmas and New Year's! *Saluth!*"

"*Salud*," says the Australian banker.

"Jesus. Mr. Correcto," says Randy.

"*Doctor* Correcto," corrects the Australian. "I have a PhD."

"La di da," says Randy. "I also have a PhC."

"*D*," says the Australian.

"Fuck you ," announces Randy. "And the kangaroo you rode in on."

"It's February," someone says quietly. "The holidays were weeks ago. Why is this *happening*?"

Randy remains standing on the kitchen chair. The applause dies down. Randy glances around.

"No questions?"

The partiers shake their head in unison, as if to say, *No, Randy. We just want to party our A's off in your amazing $950,000 town home!*

"Well, I guess I do have one question," says Harriet. "I'd like to know why you're wearing a Navy uniform? Especially if you've never been in the Navy."

"Leave it alone," replies a bald-headed young man, standing next to another bald-headed young man, both wearing tight cashmere sweaters and crisp slacks. "Who cares?"

"With a SEAL trident, no less," continues Harriet. "That's . . . . that's *something*."

"As you may or may not be aware," answers Randy patiently, "I very easily could have been a Navy SEAL if I only chose to go that route. Instead, I chose to take care of my Mam-Mam. But I passed the requisite test many times. In my backyard. Besides," Randy finishes, "I'm very good Facebook friends with a few Navy SEALS. And I wear this outfit to honor them. And I happen to look very striking in dress whites."

"My ex would be thrilled to hear about all this," says Harriet. "He's a former Navy lieutenant."

"And I honor his brave and uncompromising duty to our country," declares Randy formally.

"He died. In the first Gulf War."

"So he was the one. I honor him even more deeply."

"Let's get on with this," mumbles one of the bald-headed men.

158

"Where's Mary Mary?" asks Randy, glancing around.

"She suffered a stroke on Tuesday," answers Leigh. "You didn't know?"

"*Shiiiiiiiiiiiiiit*," declares Randy. "That sucks. And her hot ethnic nurse? The one from the island?"

"Probably working for somebody new," explains Leigh. "Mary Mary's dead."

"Wow," says Randy. "And Roger Dodger? Party can't start without no Roger Dodger!"

The guests, almost in unison, glance around the kitchen and the living room. The Dodger is nowhere to be seen.

"Let's just start anyway," says Leigh. "*Please*."

"Not so fast, kemosahbe," says Randy. "The Dodger is an integral part of our development family."

"More like *developmental*," says someone, although it can't be clear who. Suddenly, Roger the Dodger appears, barreling into the room. "Sorry, Randy! Sorry, Randy! I have a *question* for you now!"

Randy looks very surprised. "I'm *very* surprised! Sure, Roger Dodger! I'm *very* surprised! What might the question be?"

Roger's brows furrow in tremendous concentration. "Will you, will you, will you ever consider being the president again? You know? Again? Because we love you so so *so* much!"

"Interesting," answers Randy. "Very . . . interesting question. And *well put*. I wasn't expecting that question. I . . . I never contemplated as much. But let me just ask: Might there be anything in the bylaws that would preclude me from running again and not waiting another year?"

"No!" Roger yells. He pumps his fists in the air. "*No way!*"

"Oh for god's sake," exclaims Nora from the corner. "Are you fucking kidding me?! You're using this poor kid to do your bidding?"

Randy makes a sad face. "I'm afraid that Roger might know more about the bylaws than anyone else here, Nora. He's very rarely wrong. And he's hardly a kid. He's twenty-three."

"*Rarely wrong*? He has the IQ of a sweet potato!" screams Nora.

"Hurtful," says Randy. "That's very hurtful, Nora. I love sweet potatoes. And I love the Dodger. He's sweet. Like a sweet potato."

"Cut the shit! I'm the president!" says Nora, not very convincingly. "And that's it. *Jesus!*"

"True," replies Randy patiently. "But I propose we take another vote. Just, I don't know. To be *sure* . . ."

"It wouldn't hurt, Nora," says Bam Bam.

"Yeah, just a quick vote," adds Leigh. "It really wouldn't do any harm."

"Oh, you have to be kidding me!" screams Nora. "You have got to be fucking kidding me! Is he paying you all off? He *has* to be paying you all off!"

"So let's vote," announces Randy, grandly. "Who here would like to have Randy as the development's president again? Please raise your hand."

Hands across the room shoot into the air.

"And who here would *not* like Randy to once again become president?" asks Randy.

Nora raises her hand and looks around. "Unbelievable," she says. "Just incredible. What did it take? *Just tell me.* If anything, just tell me how much it took. I'm *curious.*"

The room is quiet.

"Just fucking tell me!" Nora declares, loudly.

"Okay!" answers Stuart Z._____, the banker from Australia. "Randy will be paying all of our yearly dues. Okay? That's not chump change, Nora!"

Nora asks somewhat weakly: "And the mandatory flags! And funny mailboxes? You're all okay with all that shit?"

"Oh, give it a rest," says one of the bald-headed young men. "Who cares, Nora! Just fly the damned flag! And put in a funny mailbox! We're talking $6,500 a year! You have nothing better to spend it on?"

"The figure is arbitrary! He made up that amount! Under my leadership, it'll be much less!" declares Nora, defensively. "It's just fantasy!" She points to Randy. "He lives in his own goddamn world!"

Randy shakes his head. "*Nora.* Nora, my dear. That figure, that specific figure, that figure was reached after much and *careful* consideration."

"So all of you want this moron to be president again?!" asks Nora, appearing more and more desperate. It's not an attractive look. "Really? Another goddamn year with this baby buffoon?"

160

"I think we're ready," declares Randy.

Randy points to the Dodger, who presses a red button within a small black box.

"Check *this* out!" announces Randy, grinning widely.

There's a dull *pop*.

A bass-heavy and sparkled explosion reflects both sound and light off the town home's windows.

Fireworks!

"*Fireworks?*" asks Nora. "Are you fucking . . . and how much did that cost? Dear *Lord*! Is this even legal? And on a Tuesday night? Six weeks after the holidays?"

"I'd say it is *more* than legal," declares Randy. "And the price doesn't much matter, does it? From Mexico. So, actually, no. It's *not* legal. But so awesome. And cheap. You want to know why? Cause I will do *anything* for my constituents."

The colors are magical, dancing and swirling and twirling for the enjoyment of not only the development's residents, but presumably for most of Montgomery County and perhaps even observers as far south as the hills of central Virginia. Future generations will talk of these February holiday Tuesday night fireworks in awed and hushed tones.

"Bye," says Nora, making her way out the front door. "Enjoy your new president, assholes!"

She stops before exiting. "And Randy? *Fuck. You!*"

"I won't include any of that in my memoir," says Randy. "If you apologize. *Immediately.*"

"And that's another thing," says Nora, stopping. "Who is this guy! And why does he follow you around everywhere?"

"*This guy*," explains Randy, "would be my biographer, Noah. And we have so very much to write about. I will give you one more chance. Apologize. Or ye shall appear in my book as you thusly appear in thee *actual* life!"

Harriet's comfort dog, Benedict, begins to yowl with what can only be described as pure pleasure from the sounds and sights of the very noisy fireworks still crackling overhead in orgasmic, colorful release.

"Not on your life," Nora sputters.

"Looks like we're about to jump on the *SS Female*. And we're about to hit *choppy* waters," sighs Randy. A few laugh heartily. "But, Nora, I really would like to offer you a most *precious* gift—and that would be the gift of *forgiveness*."

Nora does not respond.

"How about a hug, luv?" asks Randy in a pitch-perfect British accent.

Nora gives a slight smile and exits.

"She just smiled," says Randy. "Should have pulled my 'I juss sniffin' yo butt' line before she left. *Damn*! At the next party."

"Well, it is getting late," says Bam Bam, checking his phone. "Thank you, Randy. *Fantastic* party!"

"Yeah, Randy. *Amazing* party!" announces Leigh. "Thank you so very much. What *fun*!"

Leigh's wife, still not over her initial shyness, shuffles out without so much as saying a word. Randy sometimes finds that his mere presence can be a tad intimidating to anyone who has never actually *met* him.

"I'll see about those Skins tix for you," utters Bam Bam, also making his way to the door. "And I'm *very much* looking forward to this year's 'RandyFest'!"

"Gonna have strippers again?" asks one of the two bald-headed men.

"*Hail* yeah! The hottest strippers in *all* of southern Maryland!" asserts Randy happily. "Dancing to some fresh tuneage from yours truly! Oh man! You will *love* these women!"

"Looking forward to *that*," says one of the bald-headed men.

"Yes," agrees the other. "*Most* fun indeed."

The bald-headed couple leave together.

The party has been a resounding success. From within his cage, Fugs Funny, the magical rabbit, joins Benedict in squealing and yowling in pure delight.

"I forgot to mention!" yells Randy, over the pop-pop-*poppin'* of the fireworks, "that everyone who lives in the development receives 15% off my upcoming memoir! When it comes out! Which should be really soon! It's going to be *fucking amazing*! Book party right here! So . . . thank you again for coming!"

After the last guest exits, Roger Dodger, who has been manning the front door, closes it. He pumps his fists much like a heavyweight boxing champion. "*Number one! Number one!* Number *one!* *Randy*! Number *one!*"

"C'mere," says Randy.

The Dodger follows.

"Not you, dummy. Go on and watch your cartoons."

"Can you pay me now with hugs?" asked the Dodger.

"Can't. Don't . . . have change," says Randy. "*Noah.* Follow me please."

Randy grabs a bottle of wine and two Redskins mugs. He walks past Mam-Mam's old rattan chair in the living room, past the empty lizard terrarium filled with thousands of unwashed pebbles from the Falls Road public golf course, and the plastic, multi-tiered McMansion that Turk Wiggler used to reside within.

"So I wanted to thank you for co-writing this memoir," Randy says, making his way up the stairs. "I realize you're more interested in fiction. And I know you're still working on that silly book about the kid in Spain. But let's face it: I'm helping you write your novel. And I hope another year spent writing about me might help you learn even *more* about writing. And life. More than you'd ever learn at that useless college with your stupid degree."

Randy waits for a reaction. After it arrives, he nods happily. "Good. That other book can wait. No one's going to read it. But that's okay. Everyone has a dream. Maybe one day you'll achieve it. Then again, maybe not. I know the economy ain't great out there. Rough as a whore's tongue! Either way, let's drink!"

Randy walks up one more flight of stairs and opens the door leading out to the town home's widow's walk, the railed rooftop platform that overlooks his beautiful development.

Above, the firecrackers dance and skitter to the delight of a crowd steadily gathering below on Seven Locks Road. Cars have pulled over, including a few police cruisers and fire trucks.

Randy graciously pours a glass of wine. "From a Virginia winery. The biggest. Take this. Delicious, right? Fruity. Or something. It cost a ton. Doesn't matter. Let's raise our Redskins mugs to a new year, how's that?"

Randy looks down at the development that he's "bequeefed" to his good neighbors and friends. It has, indeed, been a most amazing year. Another spectacular year lies ahead. There are *so* many plans.

And he's met a certain someone "special."

"Cheaper than April. And nice. A few days ago she told me, 'I can come over at six and fuck your brains out and then you can have your evening.' That's *considerate*. Also, she's cleaner."

"I love life," Randy continues. "I really fucking do. And life loves *me*."

Randy presses his keychain and the Hummer's horn blasts out 'Fly' by Sugar Ray. Randy sets it on "repeat." The trident insignia on Randy's uniform reflects the exploding colors above.

"It's a strange feeling to know that this development wouldn't exist without me. I'm just getting started. God, I wouldn't want to be anyone else! If I was somebody else, then who in the fuck would ever be Dandy Randy? No one! And I will *never* stop. *Ever! Never ever ever ever ever ever ever!* Never! *I'm just gonna keep going and going and going and going!* Okay, let's end this. I'm cold. And I have to watch TV. Pop it and *drop* it!"

Randy retreats back into his luxurious town home, deliciously warm and inviting, leaving his guest to stand alone outside on the platform, taking it all in.

There's still so very much to accomplish.

That much is clear.

And this great man is just getting started!

Go, go, Randy! Forever and ever onwards!

The One Place Where Randy Would *Least* Like to Die

"Jolly Roger waterpark in Ocean City, Maryland. Let me explain.

"Have you ever heard that saying, 'Life is a water flume. There are ups, there are downs, you get splashed and you get wet but then you towel off and climb back up the stairs to do it over again and then you get wet again'?

"I don't remember where it's from. *The Last Airbender?* I can't remember. Anyway, it's a great quote. Beautiful. I've always liked it very much and found it to be more than true.

"My favorite Jolly's attraction was the giant wave pool. It's like being in the ocean but without all the piss and shit. If there is piss and shit, the chlorine will take care of that.

"I'm in the pool. I'm ten. On a raft. Back then, you were allowed to bring a blow-up raft into the pool. Before the Rules Committee and the Hall Monitors took over this entire country. I'm floating and dropping, floating and dropping, just bambling the fake waves. I'm staring at the sky. I liked to look at the clouds and imagine each of them as human body parts. I *still* do that. Like that cloud resembles a breast. *That* one is an elbow. Maybe a fibula. *That* one looks exactly like the webby toes on a freak. Things like that. It's *fun!*

"I'm looking and dreaming when, out of nowhere, I find myself in the water. This isn't good. Mam-Mam never paid for swimming lessons. She thought I could figure it out myself like she had at Ol Man Rymer's Swimming Hole. Ol Man Rymer was a sick fuck and his left eye was all hibbly jibbly, but he had a great hole for swimming. People say it was the best hole for swimming. And they're saying this even though a lot of kids drowned. That's one *awesome* hole.

"Back at Jolly's, I fall off the raft. I lose consciousness. I'm out.

"I find myself floating through a long tunnel. Not a water tunnel. An *air* tunnel. It feels like I'm experiencing a giant O, which I don't feel in real life for another two years. That's when I climb and hang on to the twizzly rope in gym class. Peppery yum. Everything feels bingo gango. I feel warm. It's like I just drank a tall glass of orange juice after being crazy thirsty. I'm being sucked into this long tunnel and I don't mind. People I don't even recognize are lining the sides. Maybe they're dead? They're telling me that it's all okay: *Do not stop. Just keep flying down that tunnel toward the light.*

"I see the woman who played 'Hot Lips' on *M*A*S*H*. She's standing to the side. Not in the shitty movie but from the awesome TV show on channel 5 repeats. I've always had a crush on her. I can also see that mother from *Who's the Boss*, with the eyebrows that are brown and the hair that's blonde, which I love, because you never know what surprise you'll find down below. It's like a carnival game.

"Then I see my PopPop. I haven't seen him for so so so long. He's off to the side just. He's just as I remember him. He has a very kind look on his face. He says, 'Randy, keep going. It's *okay*. I'll be there with you.' But not with his mouth. With his mind. It's incredible.

"I feel encouraged that he's telling me to go forward. If he's saying it, then it must be okay. I won't get hurt. PopPop is watching over me.

"I do as he says. But man, something just isn't right. See, PopPop isn't dead. He's still fucking alive. So what's he doing in the magical tunnel? Why is he telling me to go forward? Is he a dick? He left Mam-Mam because he thought she was old and ugly. But would he really encourage me to fly towards my own death? What an asshole!

"Next thing I know I'm being kissed by a teenage dude by the side of the pool. On hot concrete. I'm no longer in the tunnel. He's blowing into my mouth, his breath all stinking of Cheetos. In typical circumstances, like when watching TV or the neighborhood idiot, Mitch, scream at insects, I absolutely LOVE Cheetos. It's the perfect food to eat when watching something cool take place. Not now.

"Standing next to this dude lifeguard is a beautiful girl lifeguard. Any reason *she* couldn't have given me CPR? It had to be this ass? The guy goes to touch my stomach but before he does, I roll over and barf out pool water. The crowd is grossed out. Some applaud. I'm not sure what the girl lifeguard does. Maybe she feel sorry for me, which isn't always a bad thing.

"*Whammo!* I punch the dude lifeguard in the dazzlers. Someone says, '*That guy just saved your life!*' The lifeguard scrunches over and falls to the ground. The female lifeguard *tsks-tsks* that way hot lifeguards do. I leave quickly. Even then, at twelve, there's a mystery about me. I come and go as I please. I'm a phantom. I play it all cool. Mam-Mam picks me up outside the entrance but she's late, so I have to wait. That's uncomfortable. I see a lot of people who've just witnessed me nearly drown. Some even imitate me barfing. That's uncomfortable. The dude lifeguard limps past. He looks at me like, *Why did I just save your life?!*

"*Whatever.* Is he writing a memoir at my age, the age of thirty-four, but only looking around twenty? Didn't think so.

"My brain changed after that. It was rewired. My brain exploded into a million fragments. I became a super-hero. A *real* one. Not one of them caped fakes. I began to think differently. I began to pulsate with differentness. It ain't always easy, but it's always fun. At least for me!

"And that's where I least want to die."

How to Get in Touch with Randy

Website: http://www.ragineffininsanity.com

Email: Numberonelover453@yahoo.com

Twitter: @RandyIsDaMan

(If you send a photo proving that you purchased this book, he's liable to get back in touch more quickly or at all.)

Also: A Hollywood movie will be based on this book if anyone wants to buy the rights. Contact Randy if interested!

Put in subject line: MOVIE QUESTION FROM HOLLYWOOD

Mam-Mam's World-Famous Yum Tum Tuggerer Chicken

7 chicken breasts
3 egg yolks
½ c honey
½ tsp pepper

½ c melted butter
1 Tbl salt
1 tsp Paprika
½ cup of "secret spice"
(Old Bay)

Mix everything and then put it on the chicken pieces. Bake at 375 for 55 minutes. Down it with Natty Boh.

CPSIA information can be obtained
at www.ICGtesting.com
Printed in the USA
BVHW080800111218
535235BV00019B/1068/P